# Basic Project Techniques

## GENERAL PAINTING SUPPLIES

**BRUSHES:** 1″ Flat, synthetic; #14, #10, #8, #6, #4 Flat, synthetic; #1 Script, striper or liner, synthetic; #6 Fan, synthetic; #10 Round, synthetic; 2″ China bristle or sponge brush.

**PALETTE: Permalba Tube Acrylics;** Burnt Umber, Mars Black, Cobalt Blue, Olive Green, Burnt Sienna, Yellow Ochre, Raw Sienna, Raw Umber, Dioxazine Purple, Cad. Yellow Light, Cad. Red Light, Alizarin Crimson. **Folk Art Acrylics;** Summer Sky, Barnwood, Skintone, Slate Blue. Liquitex Gesso.

**SUPPLIES:** Wax paper palette, Palette knife, Tracing paper, Stylus, Paper towels, Matte Medium, Acrylic retarder, X-Acto knife, Fine grade sandpaper, Container for water, Graphite paper (gray or white), Sponge - 2″ square of cellulose sponge, Sponge - ″Wonder Wedge″ cosmetic sponge, 1″ bristle or sponge brush for varnish, Acrylic water base varnish, Containers for left over mixes (35mm film canisters are excellent as they seal air tight), Sharpie pen (brown), Wrico Standard Lettering pen.

## BACKGROUND PREPARATION

In painting acrylic landscapes, I use many washes and glazes. These work better over an acrylic basecoat than on bare canvas. All the paintings in this book except "Teddy's Hour" are painted on canvas prepared with Moorgard house paint, "Platinum Gray". This background preparation will often become the basis for the sky and ground. (If you wish, you may substitute Folk Art Platinum Gray for the Moorgard "Platinum Gray". Allow to dry and then seal it slightly with a coat of "Medium Mix".)

**1.** Lightly sand the canvas with fine grade sandpaper. Please use stretched canvas as the techniques work much better than on a canvas board. I prefer stretched "portrait smooth" or "ultra smooth" canvas.

**2.** Dampen the canvas with clean water using a damp cloth.

**3.** With the 2″ china bristle brush, apply a coat of Moorgard house paint "Platinum Gray" to the entire canvas. If you use a sponge brush, please apply two coats.

**4.** Allow the canvas to dry.

**5.** Transfer the design using graphite paper or white transfer paper.

## FINISHING:

**1.** Allow the painting at least 30 minutes drying time for the acrylic paint to cure.

**2.** Using a 1″ bristle brush or a 1″ sponge brush, apply a coat of acrylic water base varnish.

**3.** Allow to dry 30 minutes and apply a second coat of acrylic water base varnish.

## TERMS

**1. MEDIUM MIX** - a mixture of four oz. of Acrylic Matte Medium, four oz. of water and two oz. of tube Acrylic Retarder. SHAKE WELL to blend and shake before each use.

**2. TUBE CONSISTENCY PAINT** - paint the consistency it is when squeezed from a paint tube.

**3. CREAMY CONSISTENCY PAINT** - paint thinned to the consistency of whip cream by the addition of MEDIUM MIX using a palette knife. This should be fairly thin; the consistency of a jar or bottled acrylic.

**4. INK CONSISTENCY PAINT** - paint thinned until it is the consistency of ink or milk by the addition of water. It should contain enough pigment to still be opaque.

**5. WASH** - paint thinned to more than an ink consistency using water. The pigment should begin to separate and the paint become transparent.

**6. GLAZE** - paint so thin there is only enough pigment in it to barely tint the water.

**7. WET BRUSH** - rinse the brush in water and pull each side of the brush, once, on the edge of the water container.

**8. DAMP BRUSH** - rinse the brush in water and blot it, once, on a paper towel.

**9. MIXES, 2:1 - FOR EXAMPLE:** Phrasing such as Olive Green + Gesso (2:1) means approximately two parts of Olive Green plus one part of Gesso.

**10. SPONGE** - use a 2″ square piece of cellulose sponge for large areas and a cosmetic sponge "Wonder Wedge" for small areas. The sponge should be soft when it is dry. Pull little BB size pieces out of the sponge and shape it into a softly rounded hill. The top of the hill will be the part of the sponge that will be dabbed against the surface of the canvas. This top must have BB size holes in it. Do not wet the sponge as this thins the acrylic paint too much to be effective. Always use a dry sponge.

**11. CORNER LOADING** - load a flat brush with paint by sticking a corner in a puddle of CREAMY CONSISTENCY paint. Make short pulls in one place on the palette and the paint will fade across the bristles of the brush creating a perfect dark to medium to light blend of paint to be applied to the surface.

# Basic Project Techniques

**TECHNIQUES**

**1. LINEWORK** - Linework usually done with ink consistency paint, however, it can be accomplished with thicker or thinner paint. It is an advantage of acrylics to be able to control the lightness or darkness of your linework by the thickness or thinness of your paint. Another advantage of acrylic linework is that the pigment breaks down evenly in water so you have better line control.

**2. SCRATCHING** - Dampen the painted area with clean water using a 1″ flat brush. This will soften the paint. With the tip of the X-Acto knife scratch out highlights. If the surface dries you will need to redampen to continue scratching. As you scratch, sometimes a small roll of softened paint will form. Do not brush it off the canvas until it is dry or it may smear. Please be careful not to cut yourself while using an X-Acto knife as it is a very sharp tool.

**3. DAB** - Bounce a flat brush up and down on the corner of the brush.

**4. RUNNING WASH** - When painting the side of a building in a running WASH, work in a section no larger than 2″ at a time. If you attempt to work in an area larger than 2″, the paint may dry before you can complete the technique.

**A.** Squeeze out a puddle of paint on the palette. Add Medium Mix to the paint and thin, using a palette knife, to a CREAMY CONSISTENCY. **B.** Load a #8 flat synthetic brush with the thinned paint. **C.** Apply the paint under the eave of the roof on the side of the building for a distance of 2″. **D.** Pull the flat of a WET brush horizontally along the bottom half of the paint. Use short, little choppy pulls. This will force the water out of the brush. The water will mix with the paint on the surface and form a wash. **E.** Still pulling the brush horizontally in little choppy pulls, move the WASH vertically down the wall of the barn. It should be very wet. Make sure you go all the way across the bottom of the paint strip before moving the WASH down vertically. This will help keep the lower edge of the paint from drying out. **F.** Develope dark, medium and light values from the top down. Actually leave some spaces of background uncovered in the lighter areas. If the WASH appears too dark, blot it with a finger or a paper towel to remove some WASH. If the WASH appears too light, add some more paint to it. This should have a very loose, spacy look to it with good value development. **G.** Continue working in 2″ sections until the area is completed. **H.** Let me offer some advice if the 2″ section of paint dried before it could be completed. Try one of the following:

- Add a little more Medium Mix to the paint.
- Apply a thicker layer of paint to the section.
- Use a wetter brush.

**5. FOLIAGE** - Paint the foliage from light to dark in successive layers of color. Each layer must be dry before you begin the next layer. You may use a hair dryer to speed drying time. **A.** Prepare a puddle of an opaque mix on the palette. (For example, Gesso + Olive Green (1:1) **B.** Thin the mix with Medium Mix to a CREAMY CONSISTENCY. **C.** Using a #8 flat brush, apply the mix from the horizon line 2/3 of the way up to the top line of the foliage unit. Paint a section no larger than 2″ wide. **D.** With a WET brush, dab up and down on the corner of the brush all the way across the top line of the mix. The water in the brush will mix with the paint on the surface and form a WASH. **E.** Still dabbing on the corner of the brush, dab the WASH upward and create a tree shape. Turn the brush SLIGHTLY to the left and right as you dab to create a foliage look. Build the tree shape at least ¼″ higher than the foliage line. If the graphite line still shows when the painting is finished it can be erased with a pencil eraser. **F.** Now, dab the brush in the bottom part of the section to break up the paint and create a look of foliage. As you dab, move slightly upward to blend into the bottom of the light, upper section. Develop the section into dark, medium and light values with the dark at the base and the light at the top. **G.** Touch the chisel edge of a DAMP brush into the bottom edge of the section and pull out some of of the paint to soften the bottom of the foliage unit.

The water in the brush should thin paint to a WASH. Pull the wash in the direction of the ground lines and fade it out. Rinse the brush again and use a clean, damp brush to fade it out, if necessary. This is the basis of the ground that will be developed later.

There are more layers to be added to the foliage area, but let me offer some advice if the 2″ section of foliage dried before it could be completed. Try one of the following:

- Add a little more Medium mix to the mix.
- Apply a thicker layer of mix to the section.
- Use a wetter brush.

When the 2″ section of foliage is completed, continue painting in small sections until the foliage areas are established. **H.** Using a #8 flat brush, thin a dark transparent color (for example Olive Green) down with water to an INK CONSISTENCY. You may use the brush to thin the paint, but when the paint is the correct consistency you must blot the brush to remove the excess water it has absorbed. Then reload the brush with the INK CONSISTENCY paint. **I.** Intensify the foliage area by applying the ink consistency paint to the lower ½ of the foliage unit. You may apply it to a 4″ wide section. **J.** Using a DAMP brush, dab the corner of the brush along the

# Basic Project Techniques

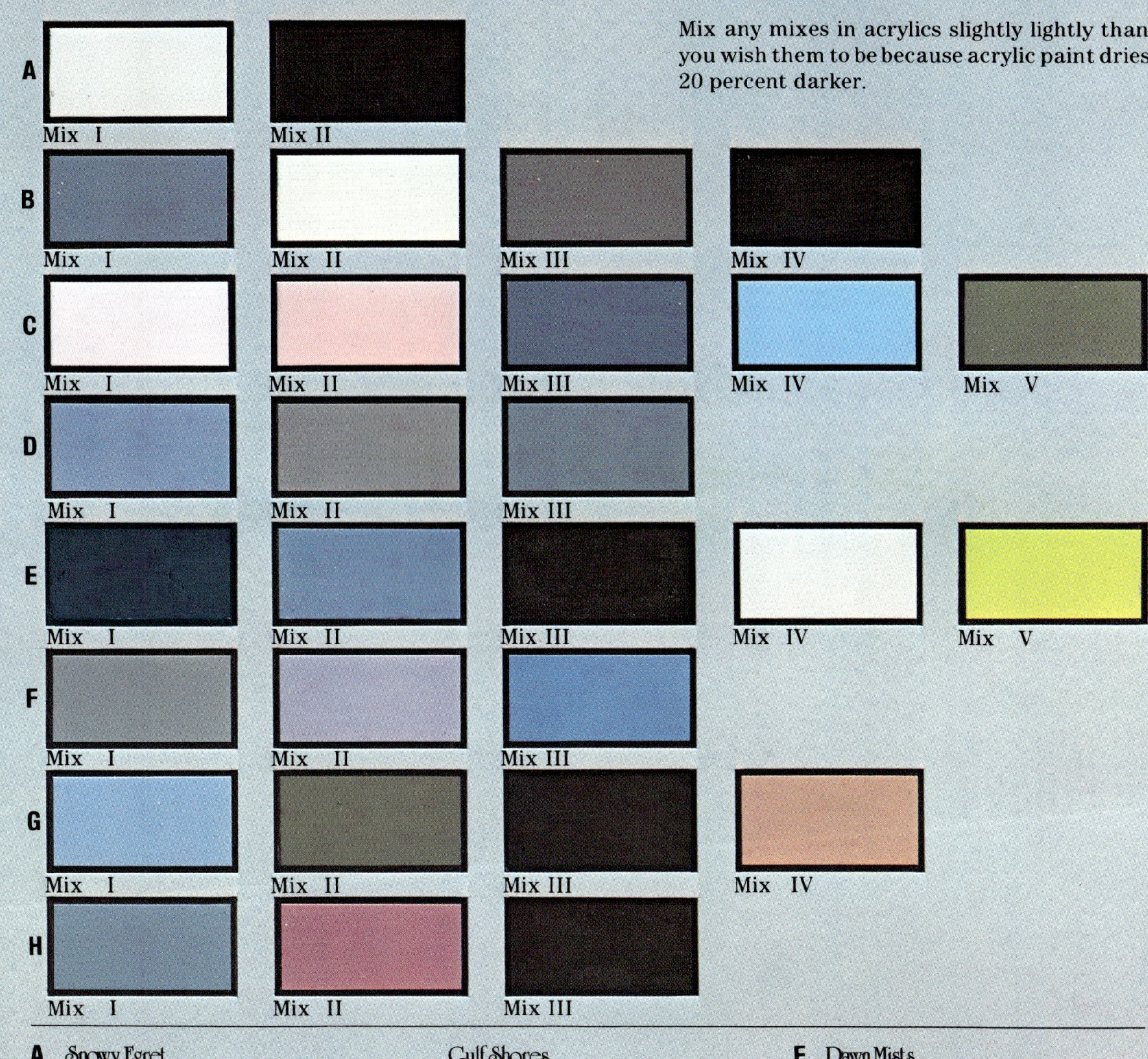

Mix any mixes in acrylics slightly lightly than you wish them to be because acrylic paint dries 20 percent darker.

**A** **Snowy Egret**
Mix  I = Gesso + Raw Sienna + Burnt Sienna + Cobalt Blue (10:1:1:1) (light gray)
Mix II = Mars Black + Burnt Umber (1:1) (brown/black)

**B** **Windy Hillside**
Mix  I = Slate Blue + Gesso (1:1) (medium blue)
Mix II = Gesso + Raw Sienna (20:1) (cream)
Mix III = Mix I + Burnt Umber (1:1) (medium brown)
Mix IV = Burnt Umber + Mars Black (1:1) (brown/black)

**C** **Gulf Shores**
Mix  I = Gesso + Cad. Red Light (12:1) (pale pink)
Mix II = Gesso + Cad. Red Light (6:1) (medium/pale pink)
Mix III = Slate Blue + Cobalt Blue + Cad. Red. Light (6:1:1) (medium/dark blue)
Mix IV = Gesso + Cobalt Blue (2:1) (light blue)

**Gulf Shores**
Mix  V = Olive Green + Mix IV (1:1) (medium green)

**D** **Morning Flight**
Mix  I = Summer Sky + Cobalt Blue + Dioxazine Purple (2:1:1) (medium blue)
Mix II = Mix I + Burnt Umber + Gesso (1:1:1) (medium brown)
Mix III = Mix I + Mars Black (2:1) (medium gray)

**E** **Swan Bridge**
Mix  I = Cobalt Blue + Mars Black (8:1) (dark blue)
Mix II = Gesso + Mix I (4:1) (medium/light blue)
Mix III = Mars Black + Burnt Umber (1:1) (brown black)
Mix IV = Gesso + Raw Sienna + Burnt Sienna + Cobalt Blue (10:1:1:1) (light gray)
Mix  V = Cad. Yellow Light + Olive Green (10:1) (light yellow green)

**F** **Dawn Mists**
Mix  I = Barnwood + Mars Black (4:1) (medium gray)
Mix  I = Gesso + Dioxazine Purple + Mix I (4:1:1) (light purple)
Mix III = Mix II + Cobalt Blue (1:1) (medium blue)

**G** **In A Hurry**
Mix  I = Gesso + Cobalt Blue + Mars Black (20:8:1) (light blue)
Mix II = Mix I + Olive Green (1:1) (medium green)
Mix III = Mars Black + Burnt Umber (1:1) (brown black)
Mix IV = Burnt Sienna + Skintone (2:1) dark flesh

**H** **Teddy's Hour**
Mix  I = Gesso + Slate Blue (1:1) (medium blue)
Mix II = Gesso + Alizarin Crimson + Burnt Umber (1:1:1) (burgandy)
Mix III = Mars Black + Burnt Umber (1:1) (brown/black)

# Basic Project Techniques

top edge of the INK CONSISTENCY paint. Dab the ink consistency paint upward no more the ¾ of the height of the foliage unit and fade it out. As before, develop dark, medium and light values. **K.** Add warmth to the foliage area by adding an accent in several places. **L.** Place the WASH of the accent color about half way up the height of the foliage unit and dab upward slightly higher than the existing foliage. If it appears too bright, dab it out with a clean DAMP brush. **M.** Add texture to a foliage area by sponging on a highlight or dark color. Dab the top of the hill of the sponge you have prepared into a puddle of paint thinned to a CREAMY CONSISTENCY with Medium Mix. Pick up a lot of paint on the sponge. Do not squeeze the sponge as you hold it. At a clean place on the palette, dab the sponge up and down a few times. This pushes that paint back into the sponge. Next, make a few light dabs in another clean place on the palette. This removes some of the excess paint. Now, dab lightly across the foliage area on the canvas. Turn the sponge in a different direction each time you dab so no pattern developes. Rinse out the sponge and dry it well. Squeeze it in a paper towel to make sure it is dry.

**6. LARGE AREA WASHES** - When handling a WASH on a large area first. This will enable you to have more time to create the desired effect. **A.** Use a clean 1″ flat brush and apply a coat a Medium Mix smoothly as you would apply varnish. **B.** While still wet, brush in either a WASH or INK CONSISTENCY paint of the desired color. **C.** With a DAMP brush, fade the paint out, if necessary.

**7. GRASS** - The grass is established using a #6 synthetic fan brush. **A.** Add Matte Medium to a puddle of paint and thin, using a palette knife to a thin, CREAMY CONSISTENCY. **B.** Load the fan brush with the thinned paint. Load the brush at least ¾ of the way up to the ferrule. **C.** Dip the corner of the brush into water and then make several pulls on the palette to blend the water into the paint in the brush. Continue dipping the corner of the brush in water and thinning the paint in the brush until the paint is an INK CONSISTENCY. It is necessary to load the brush this way so that the thicker paint higher up in the brush holds the hairs together. Then, although there is thinner paint on the ends of the brush, it does not separate into little spikes. **D.** Blot the brush once to take out the excess water. Do not wipe the paint out of the brush. **E.** Bounce the brush on the palette on the chisel edge to separate the hairs of the brush. **F.** Hold the brush perpendicular to the palette and make a few wisps to take off the excess paint. Touch the brush to the surface and wisp up and away like an airplane taking off. Also, think of dusting with a feather duster! I do not attempt to use the whole curve of the fan brush. I only use one half of the curve at a time. I find it helpful to begin at the front of the canvas when there is more paint in the brush and work towards the back as there is less paint in the brush. In addition, make the grass near the front of the canvas taller and darker, lessing as it goes back. **G.** Add some INK CONSISTENCY liner grass using a #1 script or liner brush. First pull up one grass with a slight curve and pull up another grass that crosses the first grass with more of a curve. If done quickly and loosely the result is grass with depth. **H.** When dry, dampen the grass area with clean water and scratch out highlight grass using the tip of an X-Acto knife. Use the same pattern of movement as for painting liner grass.

**8. CLOUDS** - Clouds are scumbled on to a dry surface painted with basic sky colors of your choice creating a graded effect. **A.** Load of #10 round brush with CREAMY CONSISTENCY paint. **B.** Scumble on the clouds with little round circular motions. **C.** When dry, shade the bottom of clouds with a WASH of the dark mix from the sky corner loaded on a large flat brush. **D.** Use a GLAZE of the dark mix and brush over some of the clouds at the outer edges of the painting to reduce their intensity. **E.** Highlight the tops of some of the remaining clouds with a WASH of the light mix from the sky or Gesso corner loaded on a large flat brush.

**9. STRIPING** - Several of the paintings in this book were striped using a regular width brown "Sharpie" pen and a ruler. As you work, periodically wipe the tip of the pen on paper towel dampened with fingernail polish remover. This will remove any polymer buildup from the point of the pen. The "Sharpie" pen, in any color, is permanent ink and you may varnish over it with a water base varnish. For this reason the black fine line "Sharpie" makes a very nice pen with which to sign your paintings. One of the paintings, "Teddy Hour" was striped using mixes from in the painting and a tool called the Wrico Standard Lettering pen. Fill the pen with INK CONSISTENCY paint and pull it along the edge of a raised ruler. A raised ruler is a metal ruler with cork on the back or a wooden ruler with a metal edge sticking out.

**10. SPATTERS** - Spatters help give a loose look to an area in addition to adding highlight and color. **A.** Thin some paint to an INK CONSISTENCY using an old toothbrush. Blot the brush and reload it. **C.** Flick your thumb over the bristles at the forward of the toothbrush.

**TIP**

Remember to work from light to dark in your painting and then add highlights. Do not cover up all the light color when you intensify or shade an area. Allow the light color to show and your painting will have a glow.

# Snowy Egret

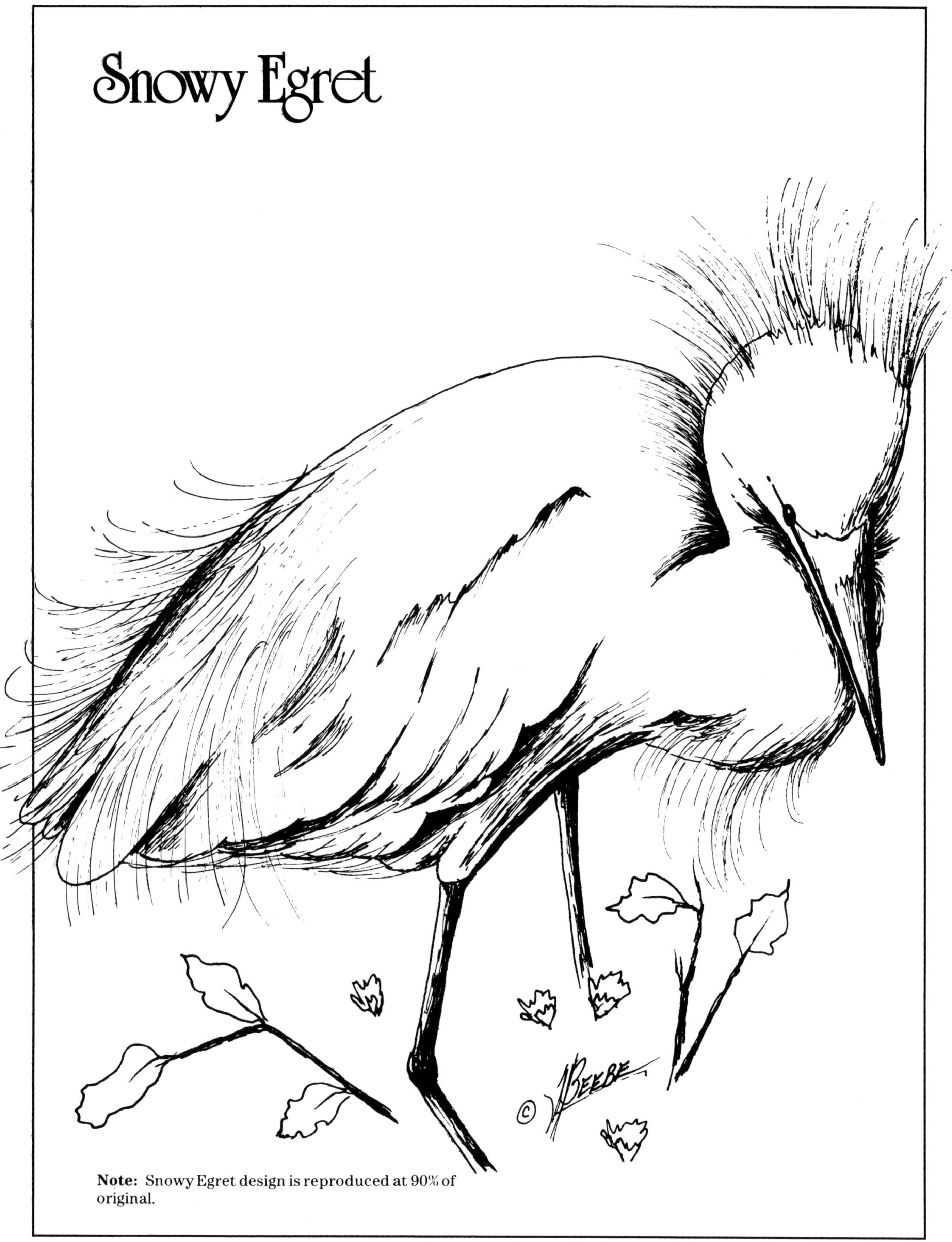

**Note:** Snowy Egret design is reproduced at 90% of original.

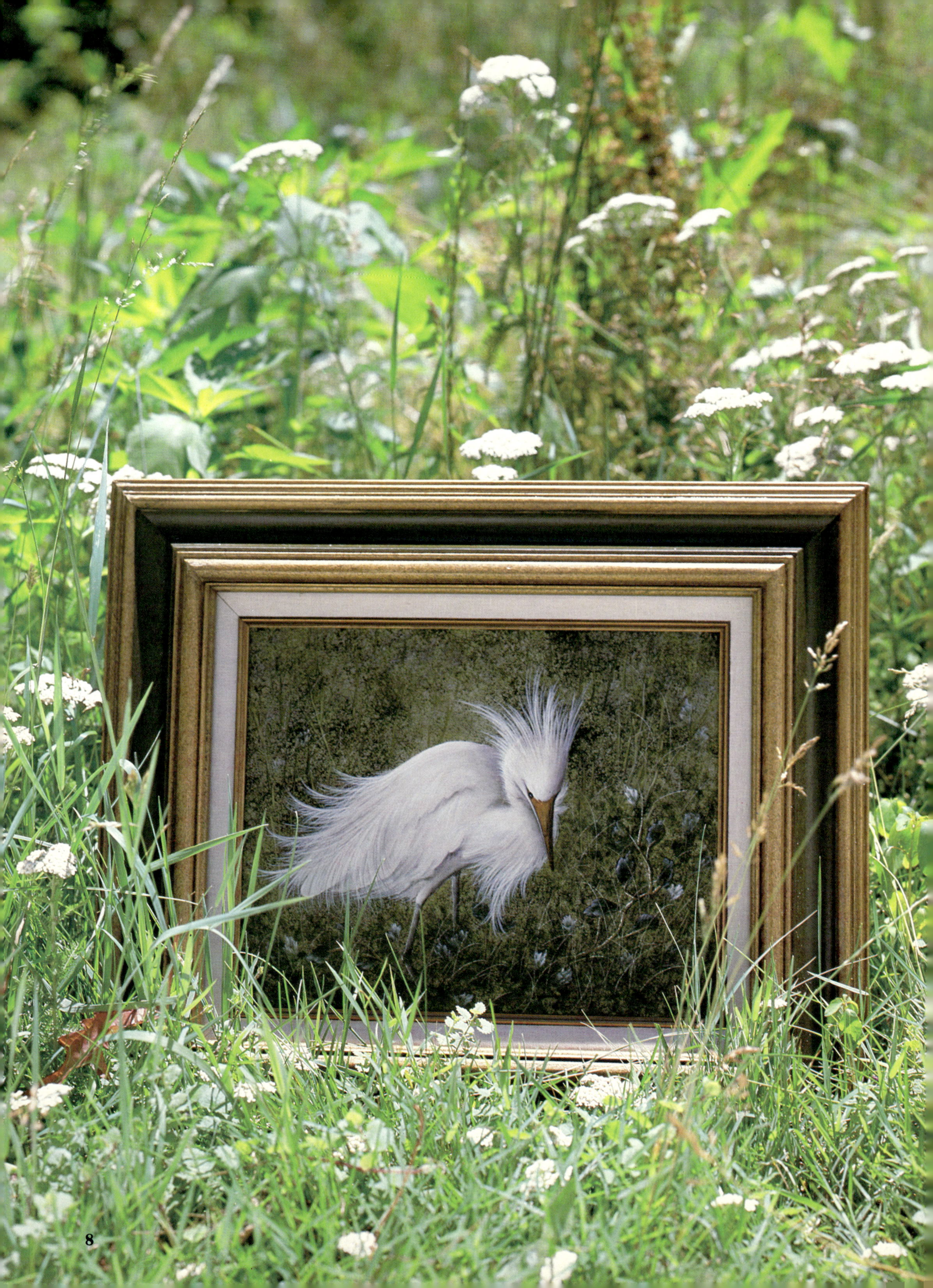

# Snowy Egret

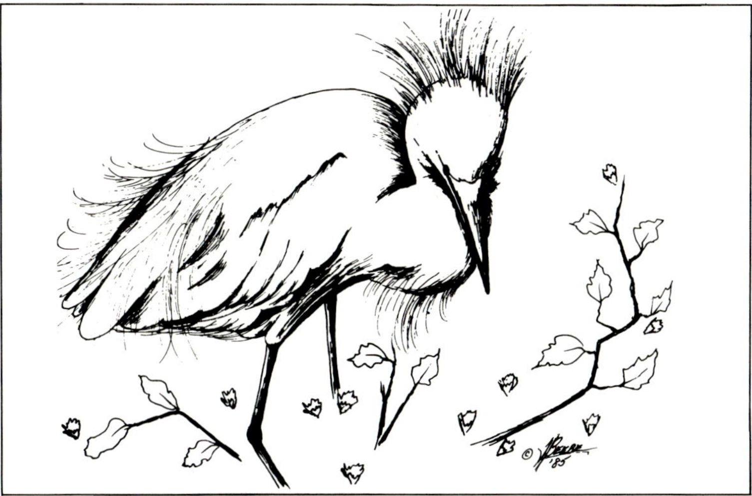

**CANVAS:** 11″ x 14″ stretched portrait smooth canvas.

**PALETTE: Permalba Tube Acrylics:**
Raw Sienna, Olive Green, Cobalt Blue, Mars Black, Burnt Sienna, Burnt Umber. Liquitex Gesso.

**PAINTING INSTRUCTIONS**

**A. BACKGROUND:**
1. Lightly sand the canvas with a piece of fine sandpaper.
2. Basecoat the canvas with a coat of Moorgard house paint, "Platinum Gray". Allow to dry.
3. Apply a coat of Medium Mix.
4. While still wet, sponge on Olive Green. With a DAMP cellulose sponge that you have prepared with BB size holes.
5. While wet, lift out some grasses with the chisel edge of the #14 flat brush.
6. As the background dries, dab in a suggestion of leaves in the lower part of the canvas, using Olive Green and the #14 brush.
7. Allow to dry and transfer the design using white transfer paper.

**B. EGRET:**
1. Basecoat the egret with Mix I.
2. Shade with a Mix II WASH in the shaded areas.
3. Accent with a Cobalt Blue GLAZE in the shaded areas near and on the head.
4. Highlight with a Gesso WASH.

**C. LEGS:**
1. Basecoat the legs with Mix I.
2. Shade with a Mix II WASH, corner loaded.
3. Scratch out a highlight on the left side of the legs.

**D. FEATHERS:**
1. Using the #1 script or liner brush, establish the feathers in INK CONSISTENCY Mix I linework.
2. Paint dark feathers of INK CONSISTENCY Mix I + Mix II. (2:1) (medium gray)
3. Add a lot of highlight feathers of INK CONSISTENCY Gesso.

**E. BEAK & EYES:**
1. Basecoat the beak with Raw Sienna.
2. When dry, shade with a Mix II WASH, corner loaded.
3. Accent with a Burnt Sienna GLAZE.
4. Paint the eyes with Mix II.
5. Highlight the left eye with Gesso.

**F. STEMS, LEAVES & FLOWERS:**
1. Paint the stems in CREAMY CONSISTENCY Raw Sienna using a liner brush.
2. Shade with Mix II WASH.
3. Scratch out a highlight on the left side.
4. Establish the leaves in CREAMY CONSISTENCY Olive Green.
5. Accent the leaves with Mix I + Cobalt Blue, corner loaded.
6. Highlight some of the leaves with Mix I.
7. Paint a suggestion of flowers with a Mix I WASH, corner loaded.
8. Highlight some of the flowers with Gesso.

**G. DETAILS:**
1. Apply a GLAZE of Cobalt Blue to the upper portion of the painting.
2. When dry, dampen the entire canvas with clean water and scratch out highlight grass using an X-Acto knife.

# Windy Hillside

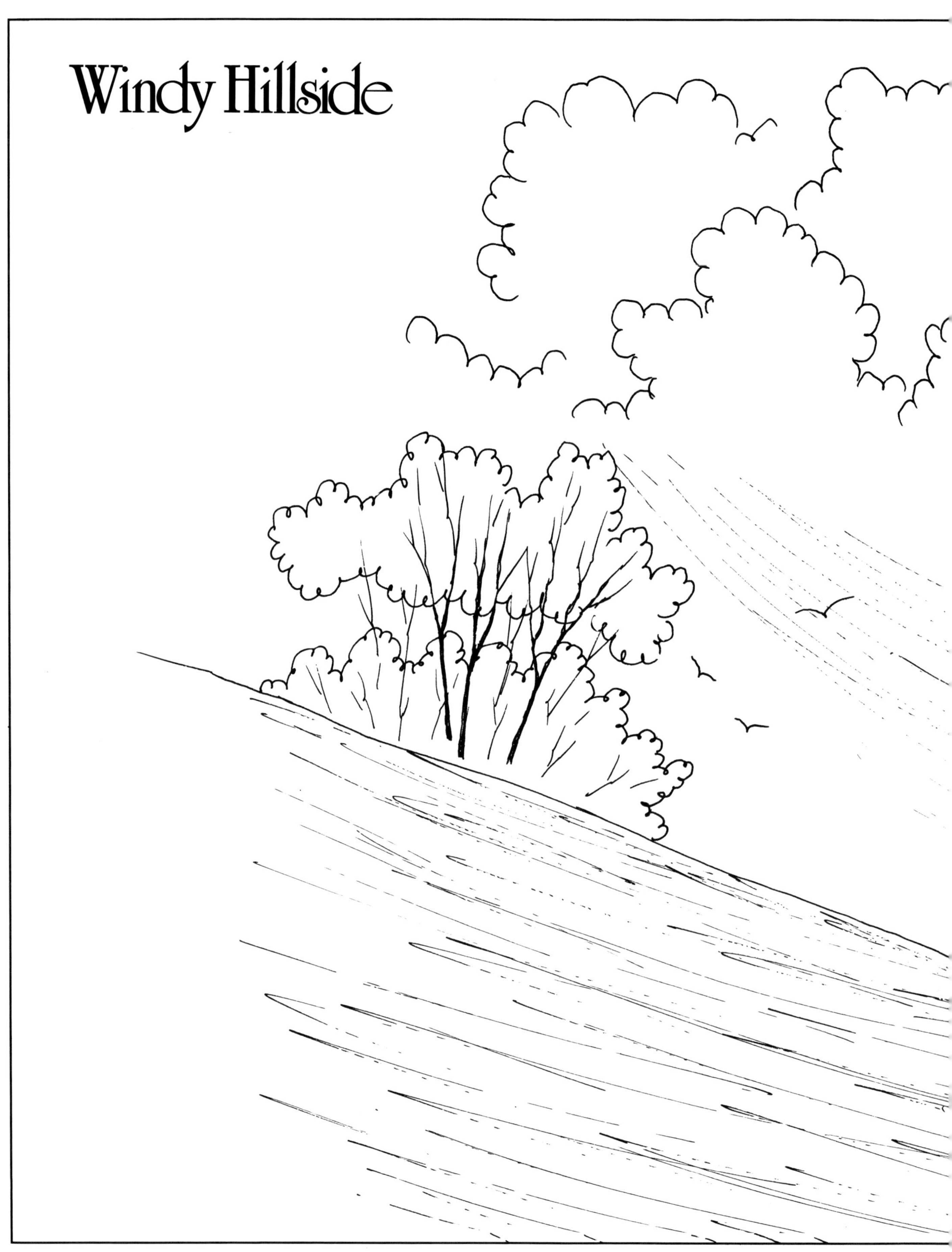

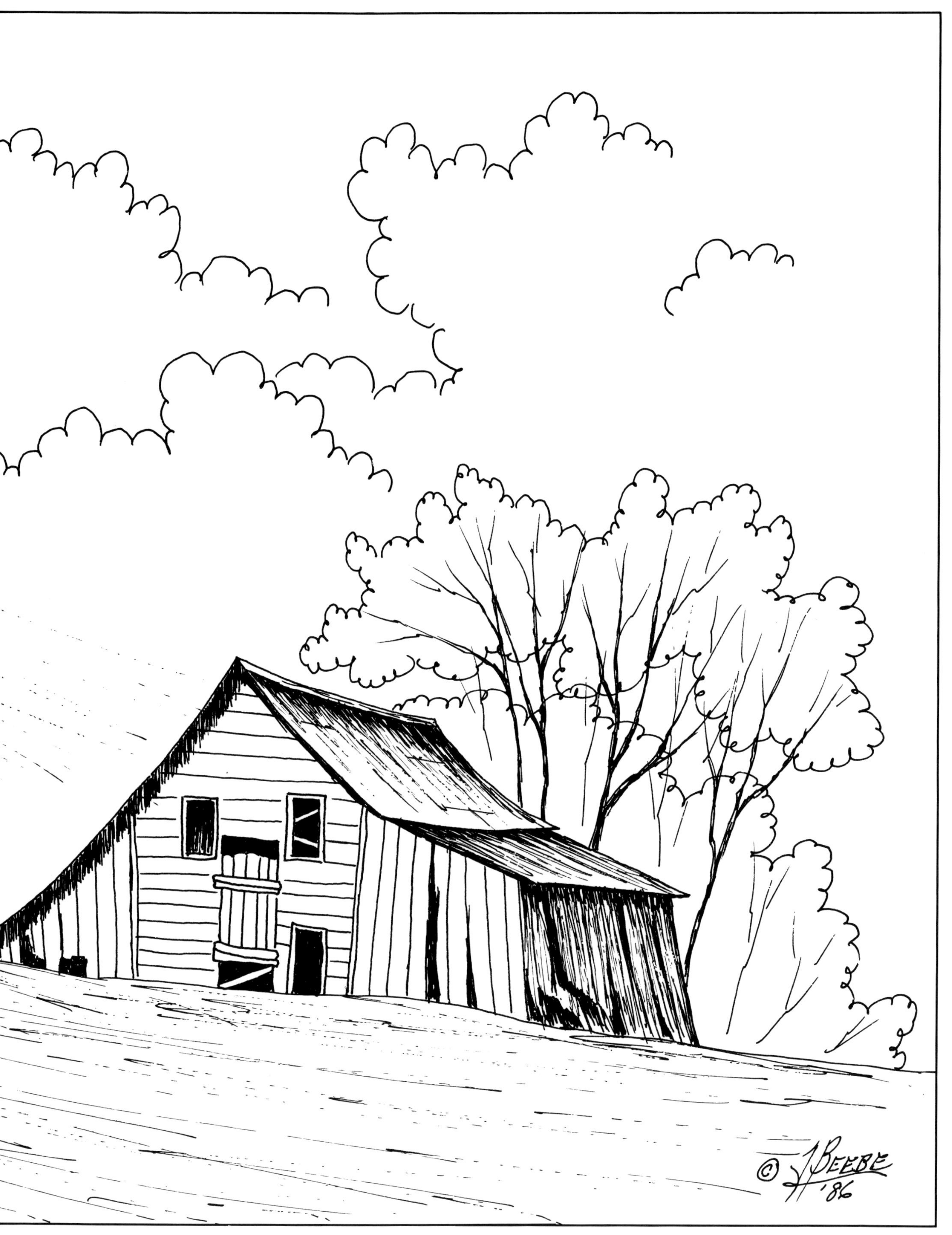

# Windy Hillside

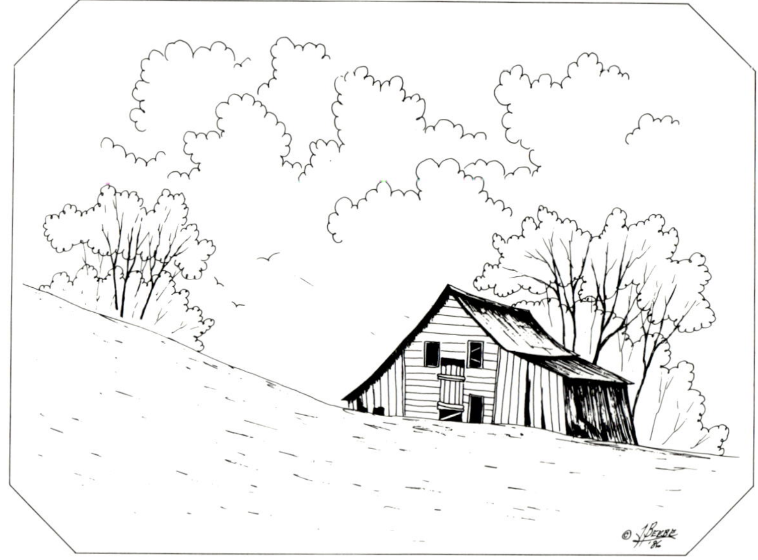

**CANVAS:**   12″ x 16″ stretched portrait smooth canvas.

**PALETTE:**   **Permalba Tube Acrylics;** Burnt Sienna, Burnt Umber, Raw Sienna, Mars Black. Liquitex Gesso **Folk Art Acrylics;** Slate Blue.

## PAINTING INSTRUCTIONS

### A. SKY:
1. Apply a coat of Medium Mix to the entire sky area using a 1″ brush.
2. Brush in INK CONSISTENCY Mix 1 and fade out the edges.
3. Scumble on clouds using Mix II and the #10 round brush.
4. Shade with a Mix I WASH.
5. Highlight with a Gesso WASH.

### B. TREES:
1. Establish the foliage in Mix III. Fade out the edges with a DAMP brush.
2. Intensify with a Burnt Umber WASH.
3. Accent the foliage near the barn with a Burnt Sienna WASH.
4. Add liner trees of INK CONSISTENCY Burnt Umber.
5. Shade the right side of some of the trees with INK CONSISTENCY Mix IV.
6. Dampen and scratch highlight the left side of the trees.
7. Spatter with Mix I.

### C. BARN:
1. Establish the barn in a running WASH of Mix IV using a # 8 flat brush. Remember to fade it down with a WET brush.
2. Add linework of INK CONSISTENCY Mix IV.
3. Scumble on clouds using Mix II and the #10 round brush.
4. Shade with a Mix I WASH.
5. Highlight with Gesso WASH.

### D. ROOF:
1. Establish with a running WASH of Mix IV.
2. Add linework of INK CONSISTENCY Mix IV.
3. Accent with a Burnt Sienna WASH.
4. Dampen and scratch highlight the foreward edge of the roof.

### E. GROUND:
1. Paint the foreground with a coat of Medium Mix using a 1″ flat brush.
2. Establish the ground using INK CONSISTENCY Mix II and #14 flat brush.
3. Intensify with a Burnt Umber WASH.
4. Wisp up grass using a #6 fan brush and INK CONSISTENCY Burnt Umber.
5. Dampen and scratch out highlight grass.
6. Spatter the ground area with Burnt Umber, Mix I and Mix II using an old toothbrush.

### F. DETAILS:
Stripe the canvas ¾″ from the outside edge including diagonal corners using a brown "Sharpie" pen.

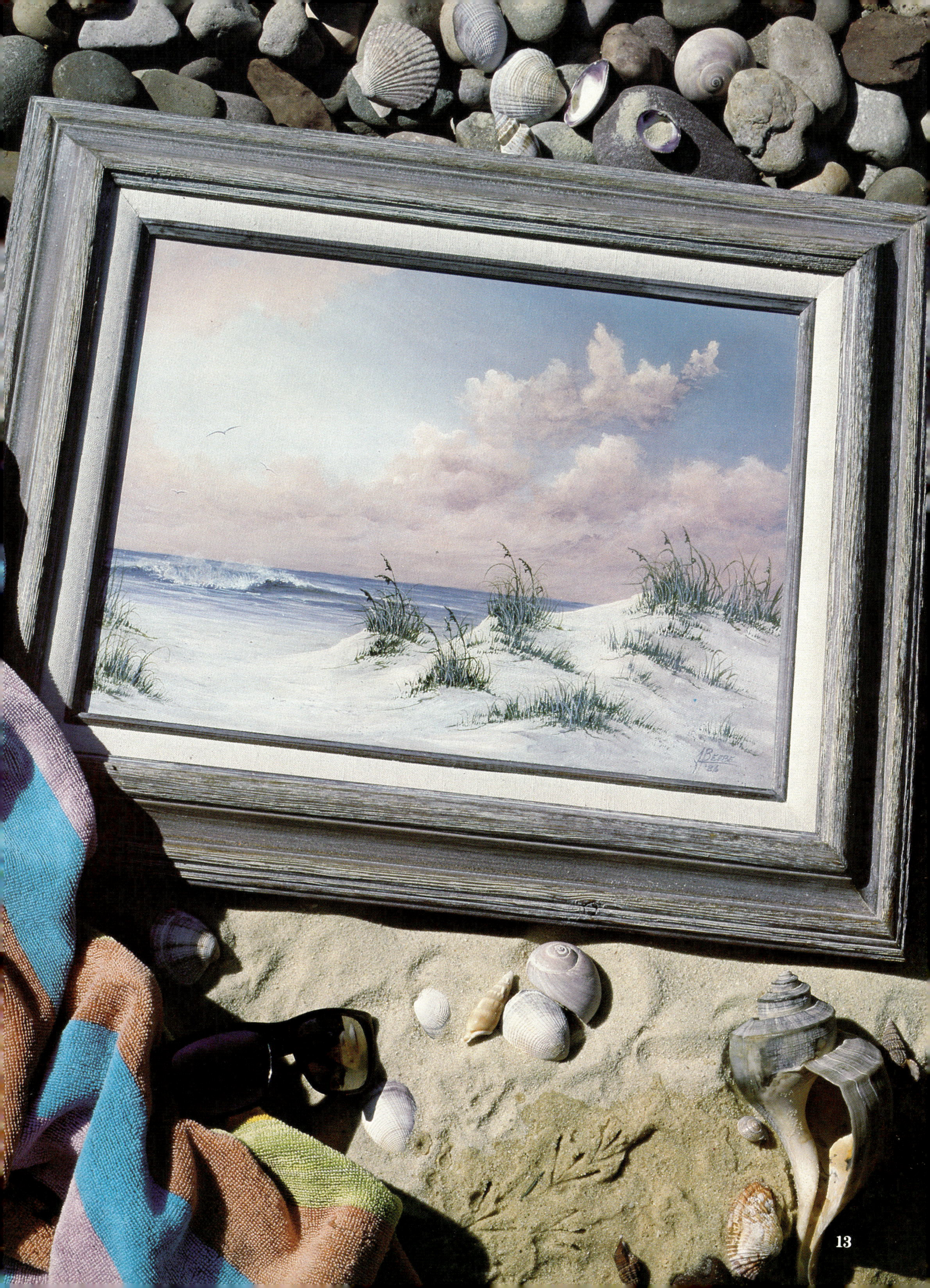

# Gulf Shores

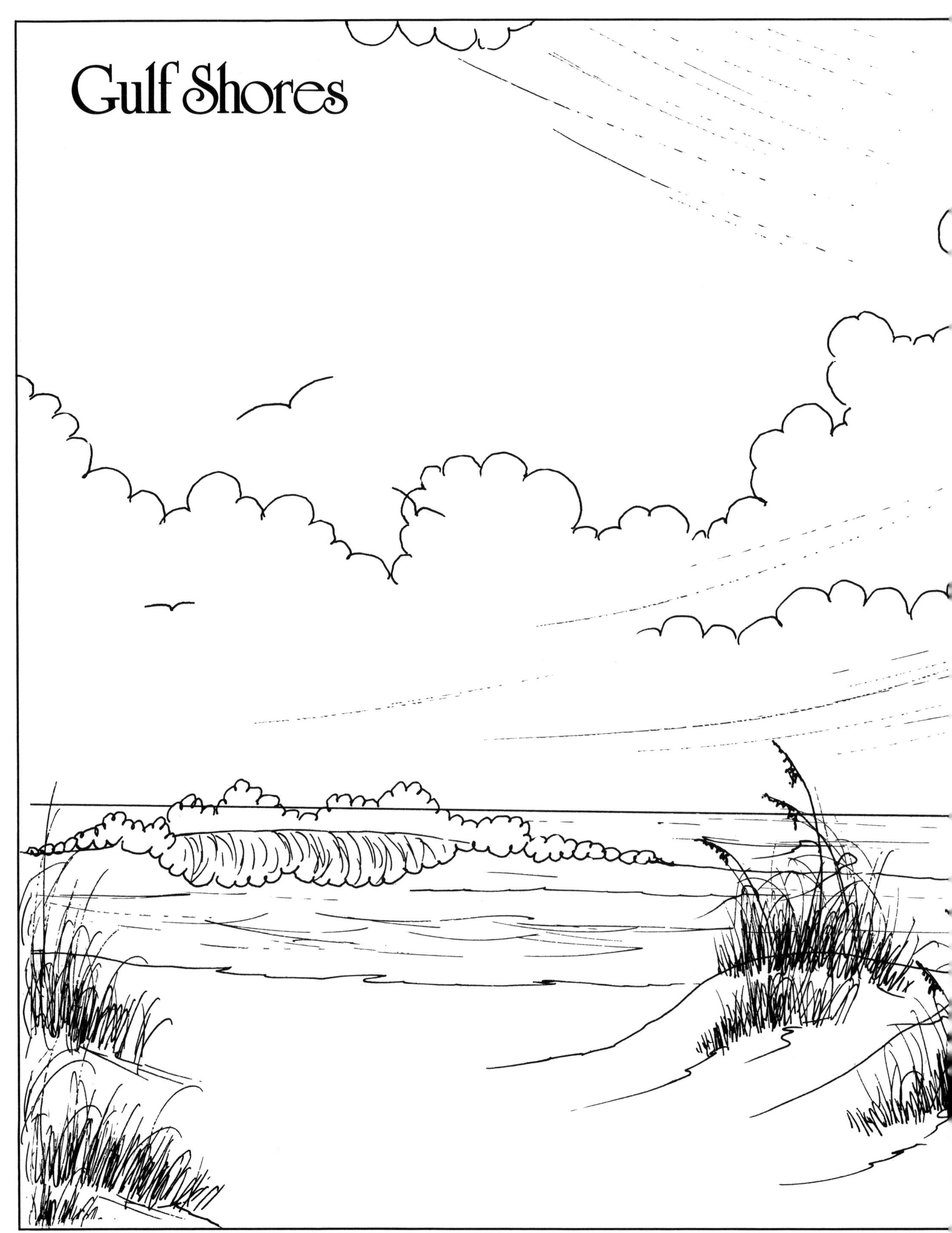

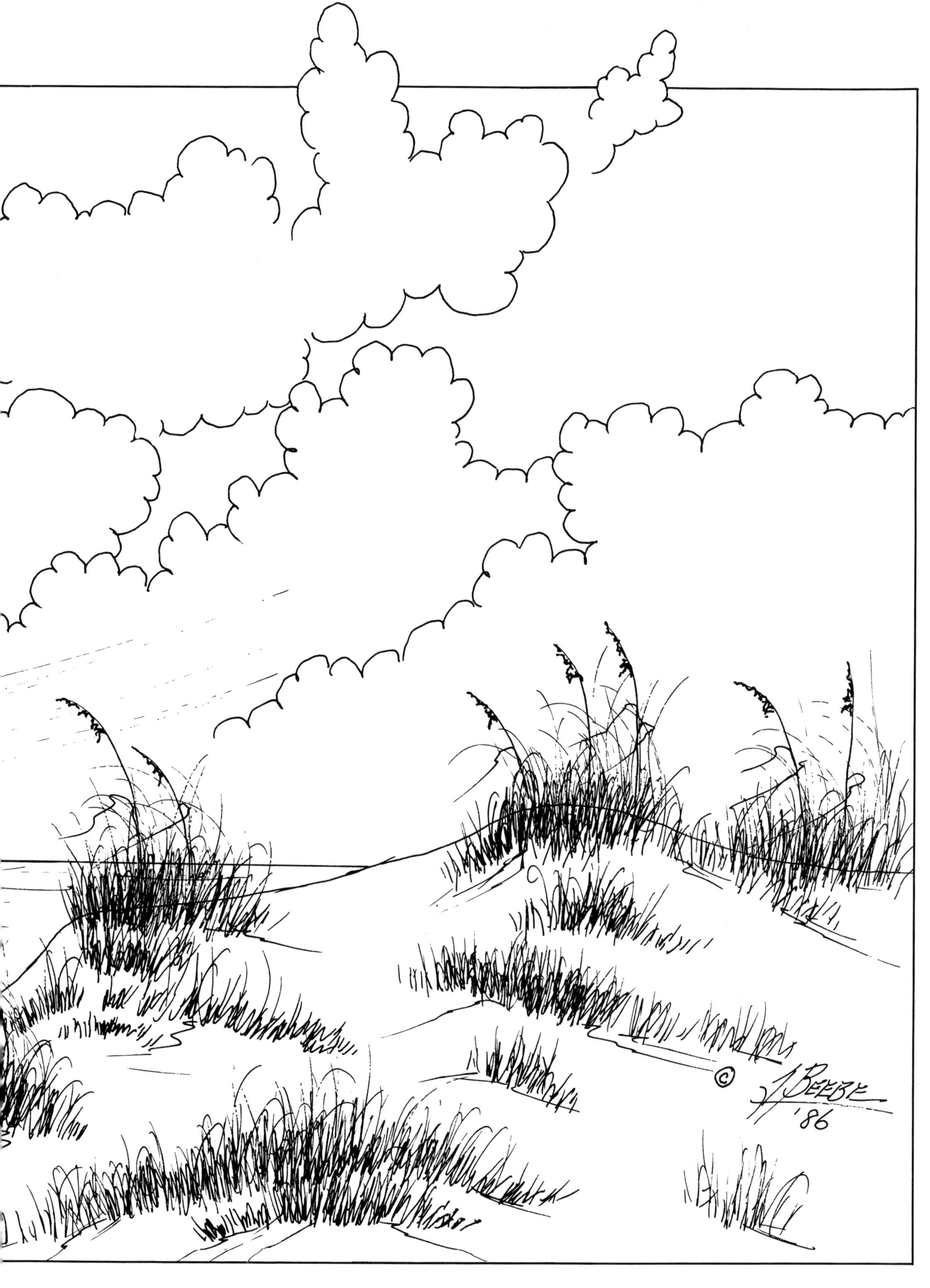

# Gulf Shores

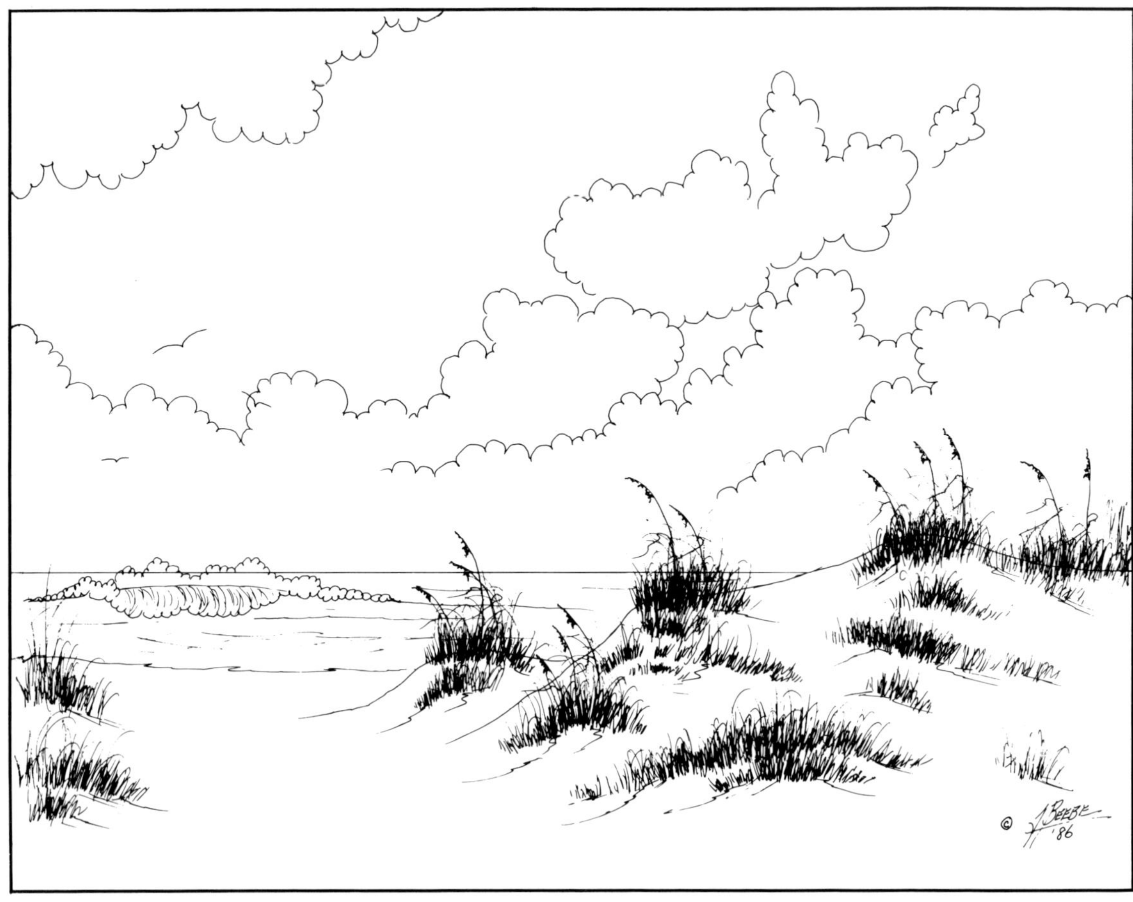

**CANVAS:** 12″ x 16″ stretched portrait smooth canvas.

**PALETTE:** **Permalba Tube Acrylics;** Cad. Red Light, Cobalt Blue, Mars Black, Olive Green. Liquitex Gesso. **Folk Art Acrylics;** Slate Blue.

## PAINTING INSTRUCTIONS

### A. SKY:
**1.** Apply a coat Medium Mix to the sky area using the 1″ brush.
**2.** Paint the upper right half of the sky with Mix III and the lower left half with Mix I. Blend these two mixes together on the diagonal across the sky for a graded effect.
**3.** When dry, brush Mix II up from the horizon line about an inch and fade out.
**4.** Using INK CONSISTENCY Mix II and the #10 round, scumble in the clouds.
**5.** Shade the clouds with a Mix III WASH.
**6.** Highlight the clouds with a Mix I WASH.

### B. WATER:
**1.** Apply a coat of Medium Mix to the water area.
**2.** Brush in Mix IV.
**3.** Shade with Mix III.
**4.** Accent with a Mix V WASH.
**5.** Highlight with Gesso.

### C. BEACH:
**1.** Paint the beach with CREAMY CONSISTENCY Mix I.
**2.** Shade with a Mix III WASH.
**3.** Highlight with a Mix II WASH.
**4.** Spatter with Mix III and Gesso.

### D. GRASS AND SEAOATS:
**1.** Establish the grass areas by wisping up INK CONSISTENCY Mix V with a fan brush.
**2.** Intensify with Olive Green.
**3.** Add liner grass and seaoats of both Mix V and Olive Green.
**4.** Add accent grass of Mix IV.
**5.** Dampen and scratch out highlight grass.

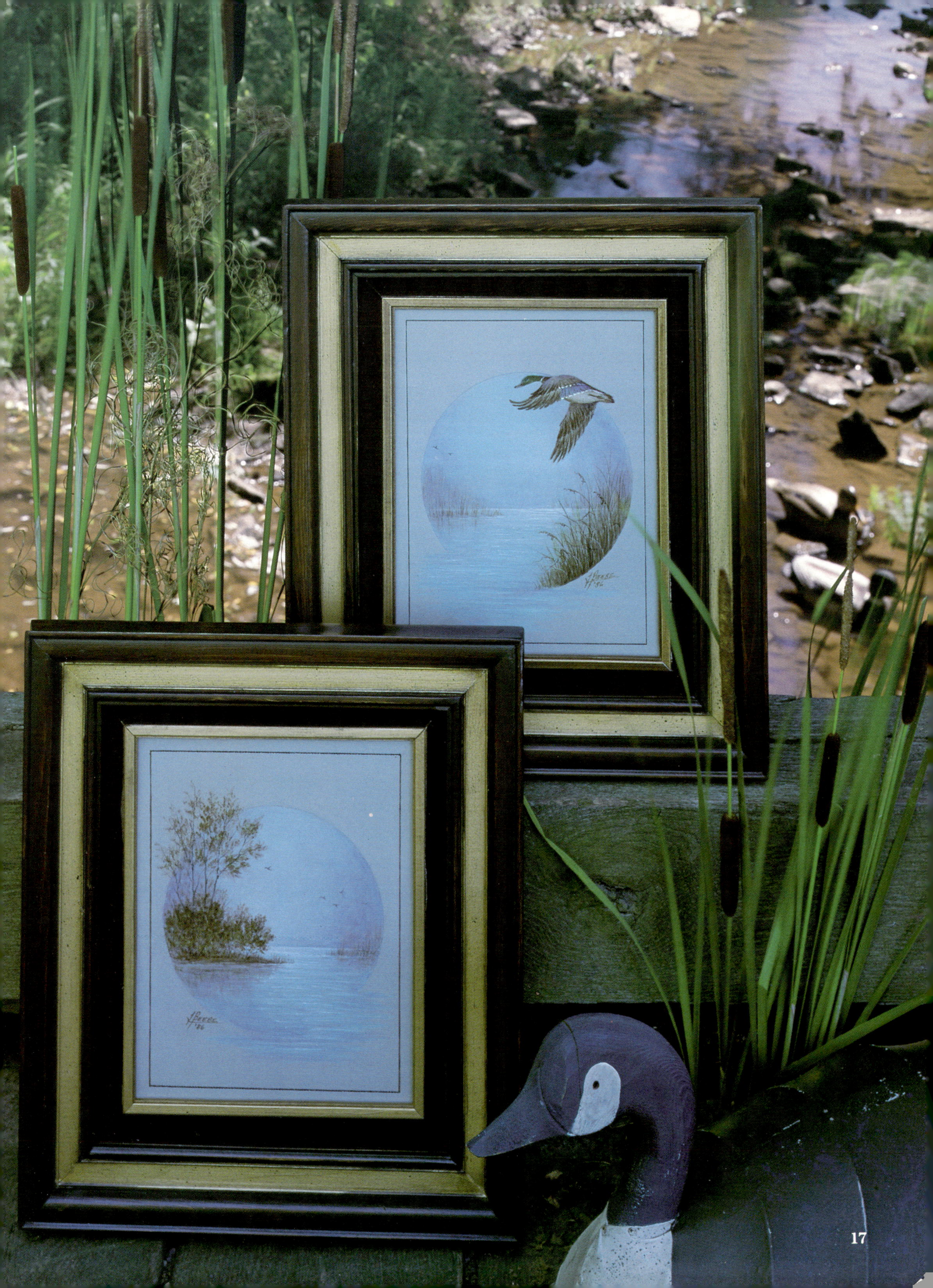

# Morning Flight

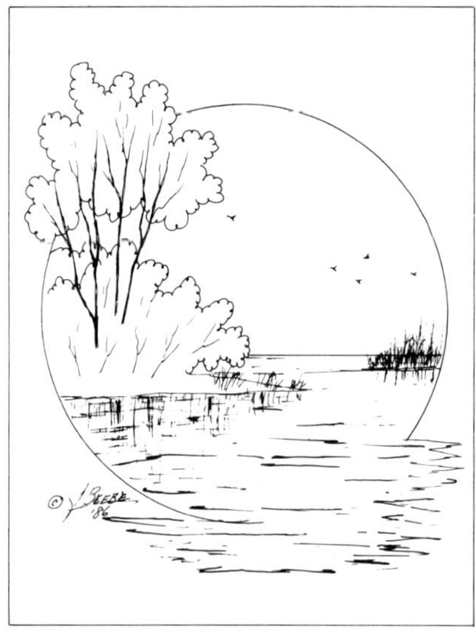 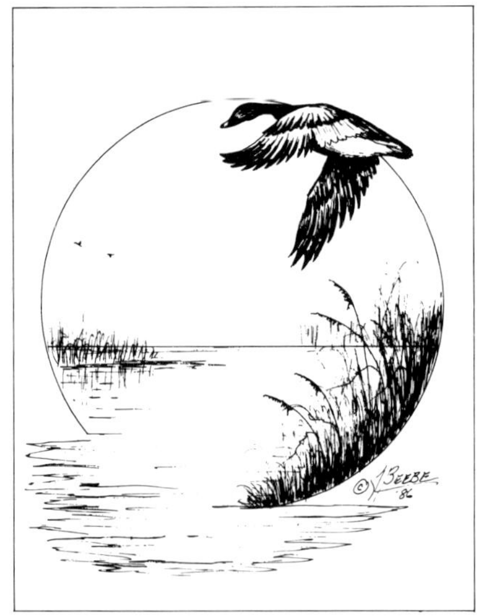

**CANVAS:** Two 8″ x 10″ stretched portrait smooth canvases.

**PALETTE:** **Permalba Tube Acrylics;** Cobalt Blue, Mars Black, Dioxazine Purple, Burnt Umber, Olive Green. Liquitex Gesso. **Folk Art Acrylics;** Summer Sky, Barnwood.

## PAINTING INSTRUCTIONS

### A. SKY AND WATER:
**1.** Apply a coat of Medium Mix to the circle using a 1″ flat brush.
**2.** Brush in INK CONSISTENCY Summer Sky evenly over the circle.
**3.** Using a #14 flat brush pull out streaks of Summer Sky from the circle to establish the water area.
**4.** Intensify each side of the sky and water with a Mix I WASH.
**5.** Intensify the same areas with a Dioxazine Purple GLAZE.
**6.** Highlight the center of the sky with a Gesso WASH.
**7.** Highlight the center of the water with streaks of INK CONSISTENCY Gesso linework.

### B. TREES AND REFLECTIONS:
**1.** Establish the foliage and reflections by dabbing in a WASH of Mix II using the corner of a #8 flat brush. Fade out with a DAMP brush.
**2.** Intensify with a Burnt Umber WASH.
**3.** Accent with an Olive Green GLAZE.

**4.** Add liner trees of INK CONSISTENCY Mars Black.

### C. GRASS AND WEEDS:
**1.** Establish the grass areas by wisping up a Mix II WASH.
**2.** Intensify with a Burnt Umber liner grass and weeds.
**3.** Accent the near grass area with an Olive Green WASH.
**4.** Dampen with clean water and scratch out highlight grass.

### D. MALLARD:
**1.** Basecoat the duck with Barnwood.
**2.** Paint the head with an Olive Green WASH.
**3.** Paint an area on the wing with CREAMY CONSISTENCY Mix I.
**4.** Shade the beak, chest, stomach and wings with a Burnt Umber WASH.
**5.** Pull on wing feathers of INK CONSISTENCY Burnt Umber using the tip of a liner brush.
**6.** Highlight the head with a Summer Sky WASH, corner loaded.
**7.** Highlight the wing with a Mix I WASH.
**8.** Add Gesso highlights to the neck and wing using the tip of a liner brush.
**9.** Accent the beak with a Gesso GLAZE, corner loaded.

### E. DETAILS:
Stripe the canvas ½″ from the outside edge with a brown "Sharpie" pen. Paint liner birds with INK CONSISTENCY Mix III.

# Morning Flight

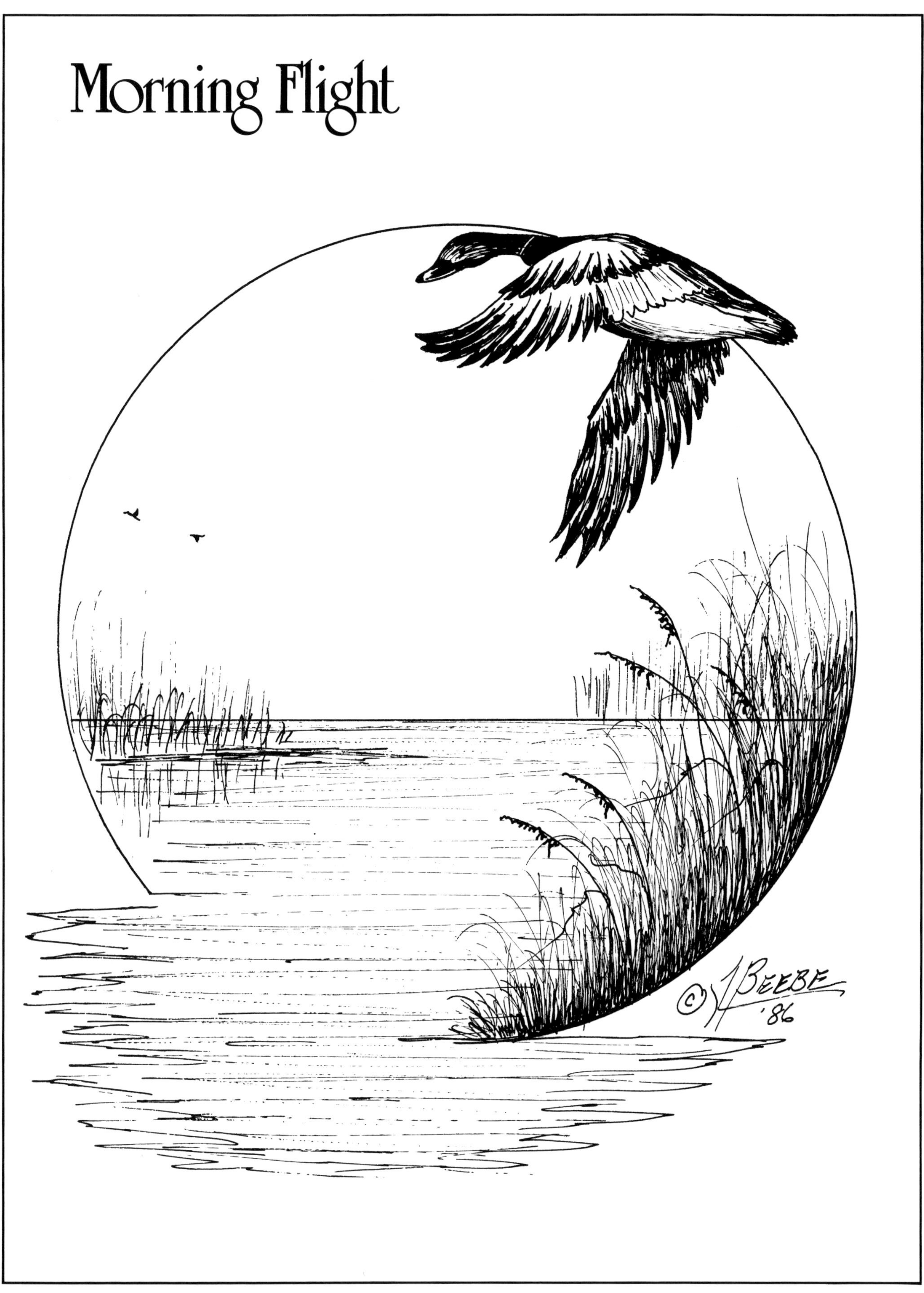

# Morning Flight

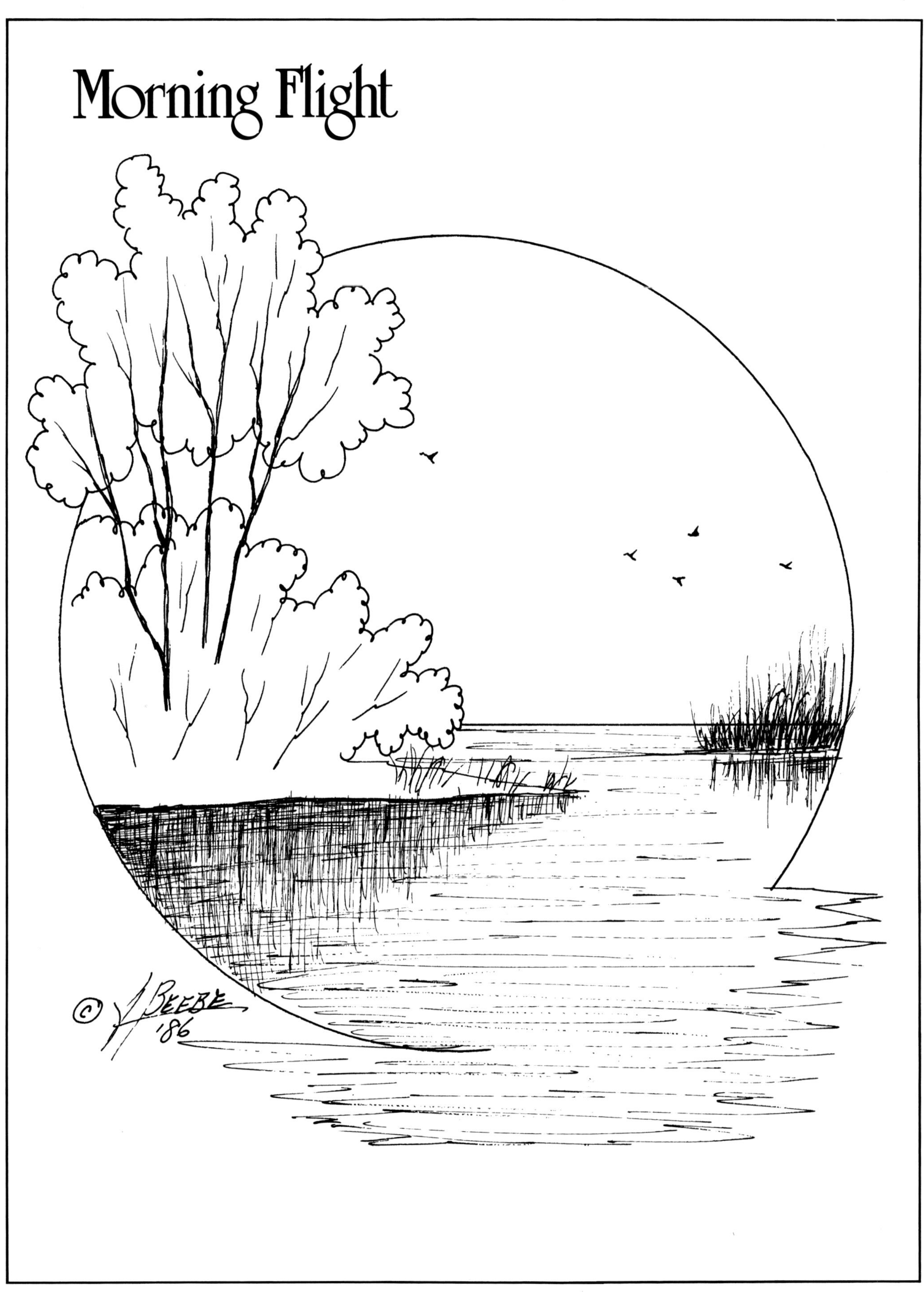

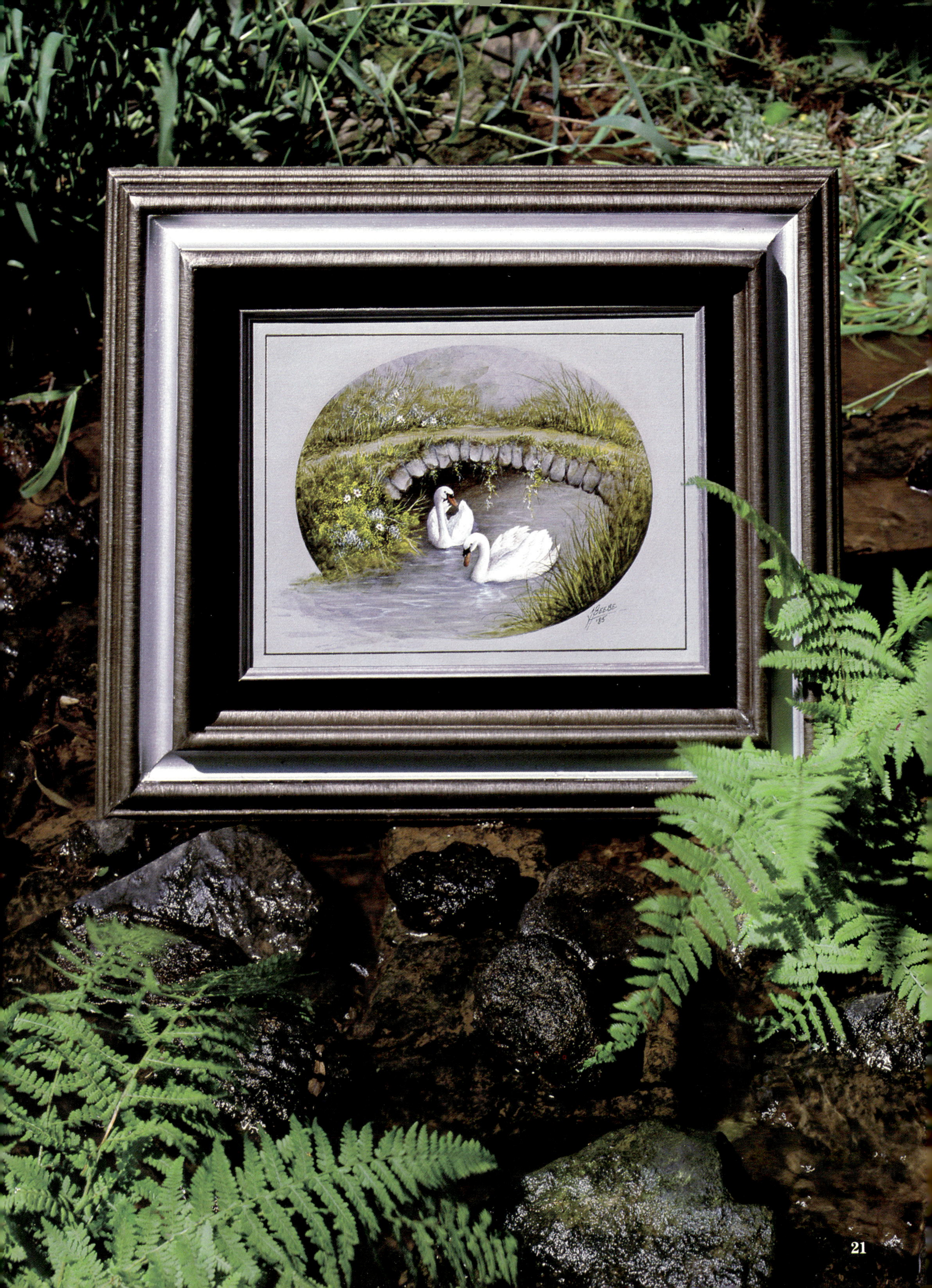

# Swan Bridge

**CANVAS:**    6″ x 12″ stretched portrait smooth canvas.

**PALETTE:**    **Permalba Tube Acrylics;** Olive Green, Raw Sienna, Burnt Sienna, Cobalt Blue, Mars Black, Burnt Umber, Cad. Yellow Light. Liquitex Gesso.

## PAINTING INSTRUCTIONS

### A. SKY AND WATER:
1. Apply a flat WASH of Mix II to the sky area.
2. Apply Mix II to the water area and streak it out of the the oval.

### B. GROUND:
1. Apply an Olive Green WASH to the ground area.
2. Wisp up INK CONSISTENCY Olive Green grass.
3. Add Olive Green liner grass.
4. Highlight with Mix V liner grass.
5. Scratch out highlight grass using an X-Acto knife.

### C. FOLIAGE:
1. Dab in CREAMY CONSISTENCY Olive Green.
2. Highlight with Mix V using a small sponge ("Wonder Wedge") you have prepared with BB size holes.

### D. ROCKS:
1. Establish the dark areas of the rocks with a Mix III WASH, corner loaded.
2. Accent with a Burnt Umber GLAZE.
3. Highlight with a Mix II GLAZE, corner loaded.
4. Soften with a Barnwood WASH if necessary.

### E. WATER:
1. Apply a coat of Medium Mix to the water area.
2. Darken under the left side of the bridge with Mix III.
3. Intensify the water with Mix I WASH.
4. Highlight with Gesso.

### F. SWANS:
1. Basecoat the swans with Mix IV.
2. Shade with a Mix III WASH, corner loaded.
3. Accent with a Mix I GLAZE in the shaded area and on the forward swan's forward wing.
4. Highlight with a Gesso WASH.
5. Paint the mandibles and eyes with Mix III and highlight with Gesso.

### G. BEAKS:
1. Basecoat with Raw Sienna.
2. Shade with a Mix III WASH, corner loaded.
3. Accent with a Burnt Sienna GLAZE.

### H. DAISIES:
1. Establish the daisies using Mix IV and the tip of a liner brush.
2. Highlight some petals with Gesso.
3. Paint the centers Raw Sienna.
4. Accent the centers with Burnt Sienna.

### I. VINES:
1. Paint the vines with Olive Green linework.
2. Highlight with Mix IV.
3. Dab on accent flowers of Mix I and Gesso.
4. Scratch highlight the vines.

### J. DETAILS:
Stripe the canvas ½″ from the outside edge using a brown "Sharpie" pen.

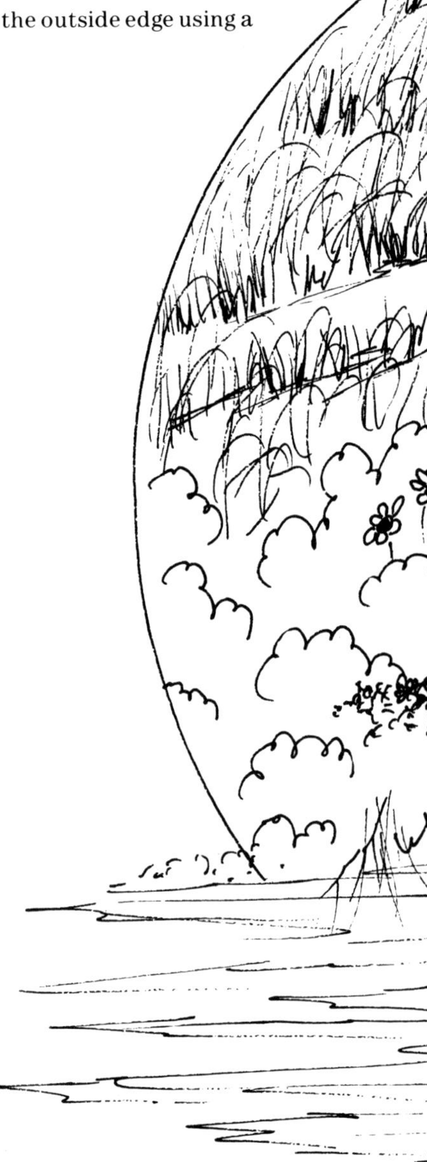

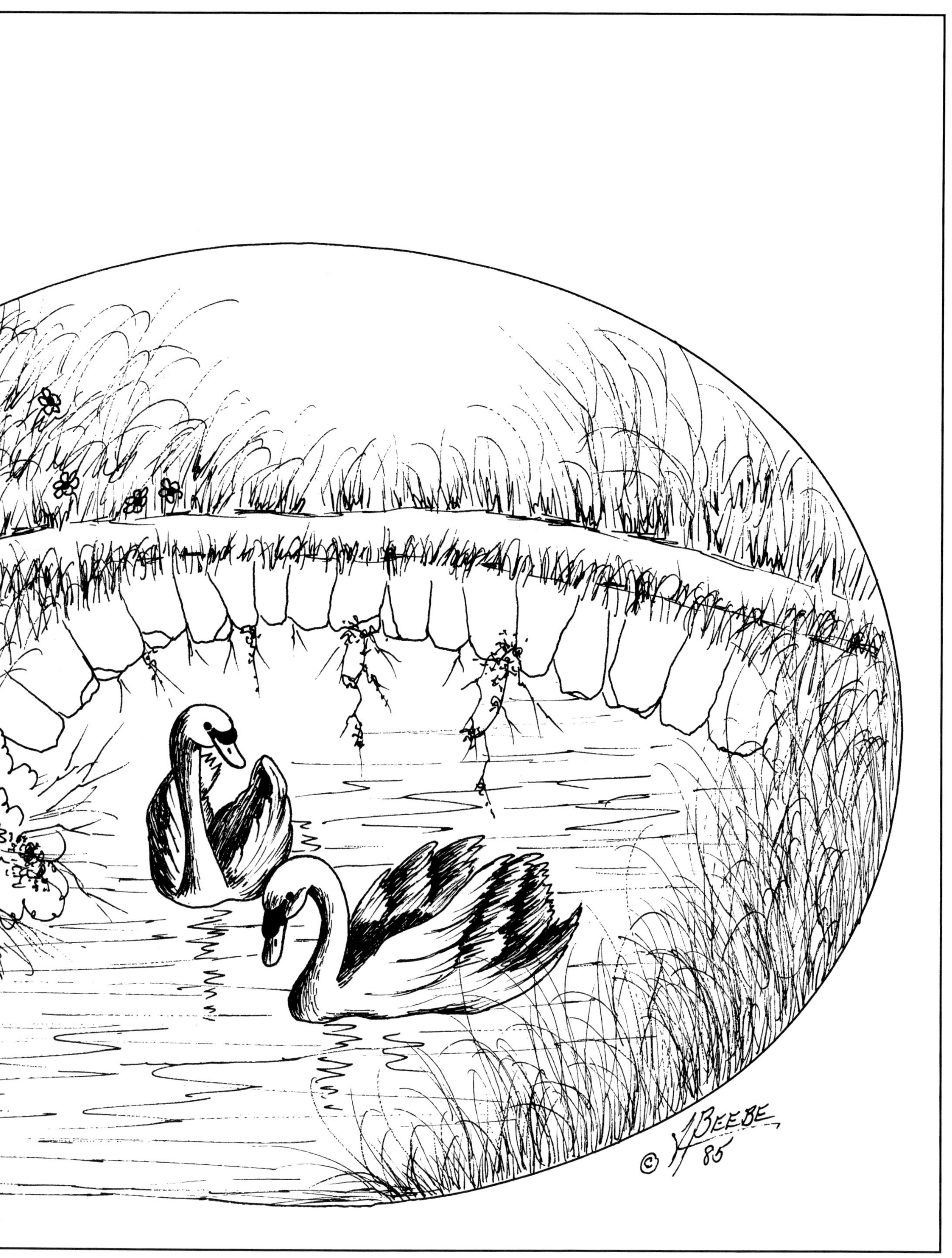

# Dawn Mists

**CANVAS:**  6″ x 12″ stretched portrait smooth canvas.

**PALETTE:**  **Permalba Tube Acrylics;** Raw Umber, Raw Sienna, Olive Green, Cobalt Blue, Mars Black, Dioxazine Purple. Liquitex Gesso. **Folk Art Acrylics;** Barnwood.

## PAINTING INSTRUCTIONS

### A. MIST:
**1.** Paint the canvas from the horizon up with a coat of Medium Mix using the 1″ flat brush.
**2.** Establish the background mist with a Gesso WASH.

### B. TREES:
**1.** Paint the trees in a Raw Umber WASH.
**2.** Shadow the right sides of the trees with a Mars Black GLAZE.

### C. DISTANT FOLIAGE:
**1.** Establish the distant foliage in CREAMY CONSISTENCY Mix I.
**2.** Intensify with an Olive Green WASH.
**3.** Add liner trees of Raw Umber + Mars Black. (1:1) (brown/black)
**4.** Dampen and scratch out highlights with an X-Acto knife.

### D. FAWN:
**1.** Basecoat the fawn in Raw Umber.
**2.** Shade with a Mars Black WASH.

### E. GROUND:
**1.** Establish the ground lines using the #14 flat brush and a WASH of Mix I.
**2.** Intensify with an Olive Green WASH.
**3.** Wisp up grass using a #6 fan brush and INK CONSISTENCY Olive Green.
**4.** Add liner grass of Olive Green.
**5.** Dampen and scratch out highlight grass with an X-Acto knife.

### F. FLOWERS:
**1.** Paint the flowers in Mix II and Mix III using the tip of a liner brush.
**2.** Add centers of Raw Sienna and some of Raw Sienna + Gesso. (1:1)
**3.** Highlight some of the flower petals with Gesso.

### G. TREE FOLIAGE:
**1.** Dab on the tree foliage in a Mix I WASH using a #8 flat brush.
**2.** Intensify with an Olive Green WASH.
**3.** Add some foliage of Olive Green and Raw Sienna.
**4.** Highlight with Raw Sienna + Gesso. (1:1)
**5.** Add accents of Mix II and Mix III.

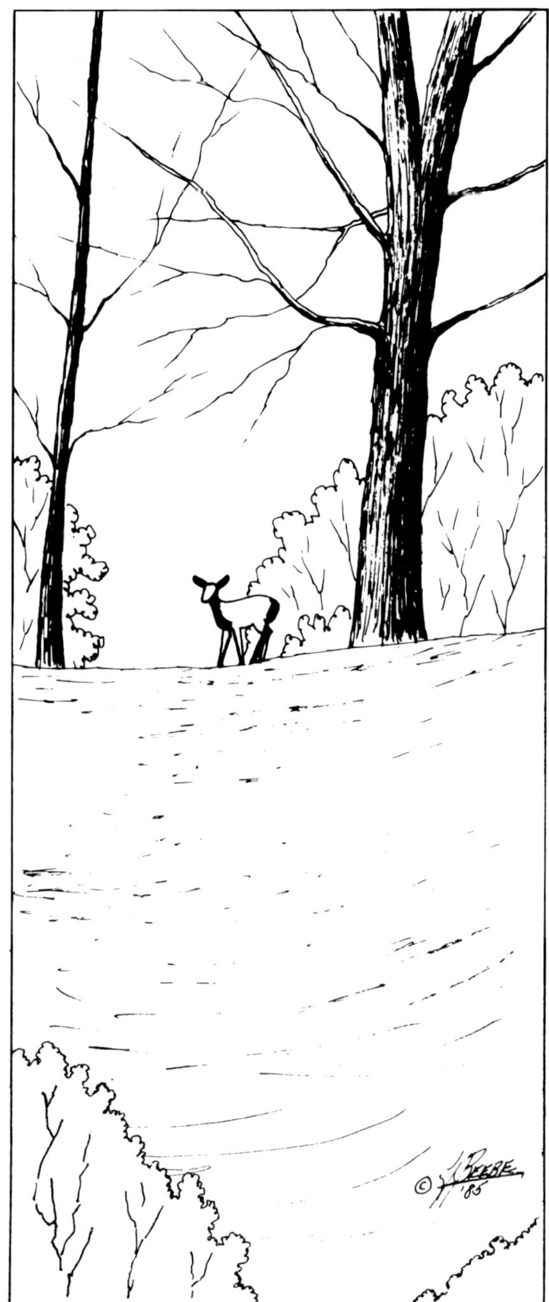

### H. DETAILS:
**1.** Paint the canvas with a coat of Medium Mix.
**2.** Apply a mist of a Gesso GLAZE to the upper 2/3 of the canvas.
**3.** Allow to dry.
**4.** Accent the mist with a Mix II GLAZE on the lower right and a Mix III GLAZE on the upper left.

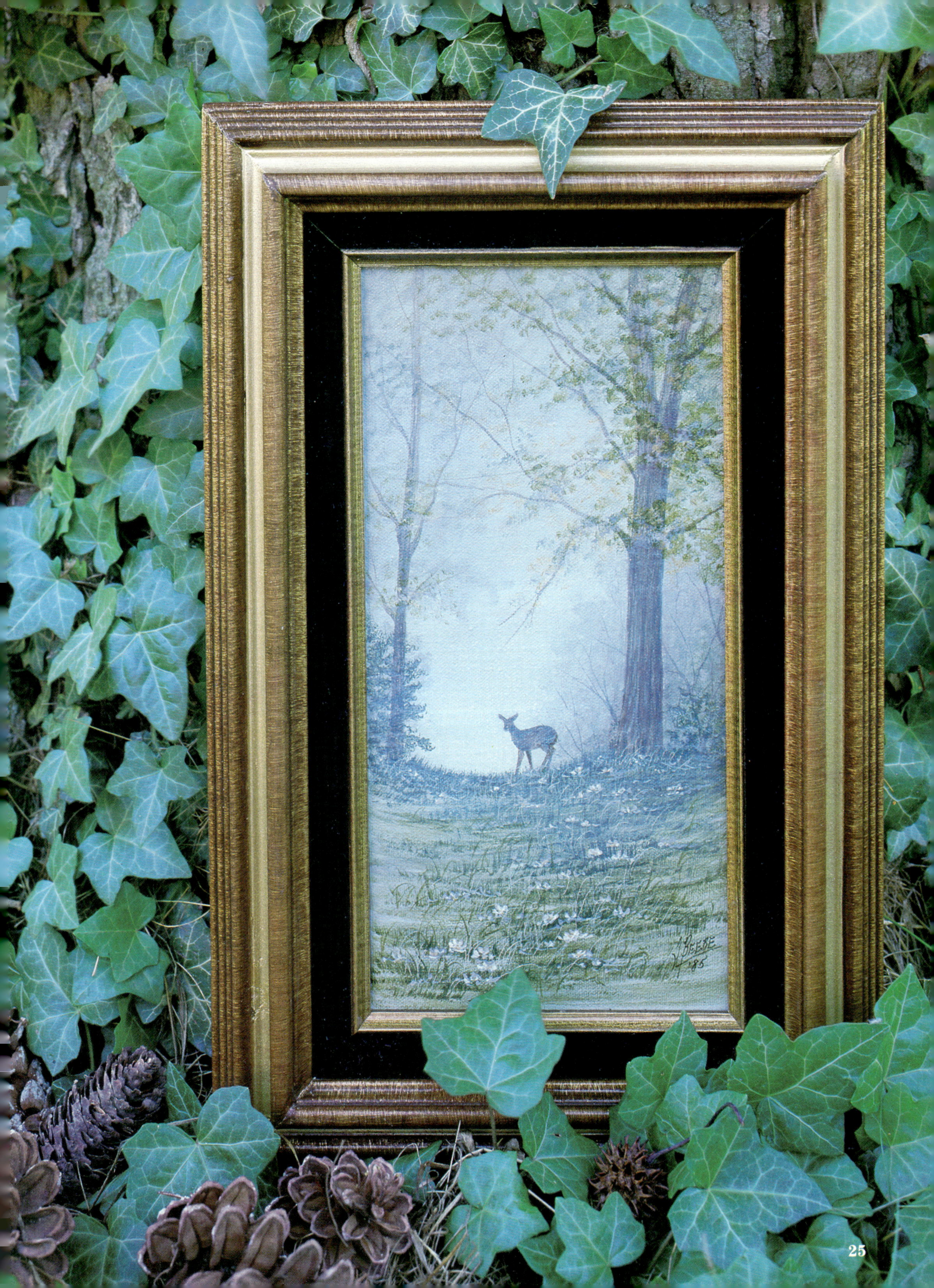

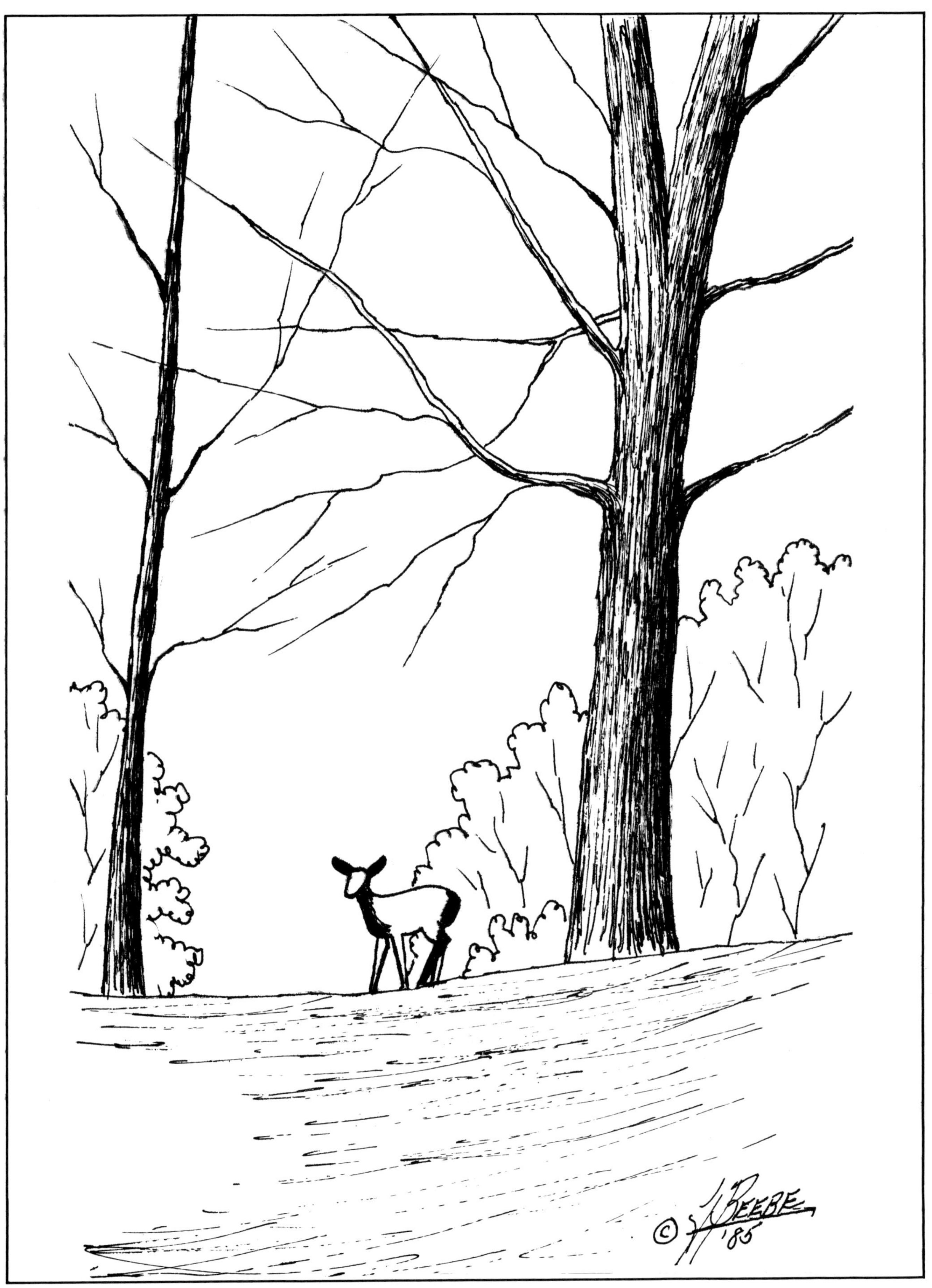

# In A Hurry

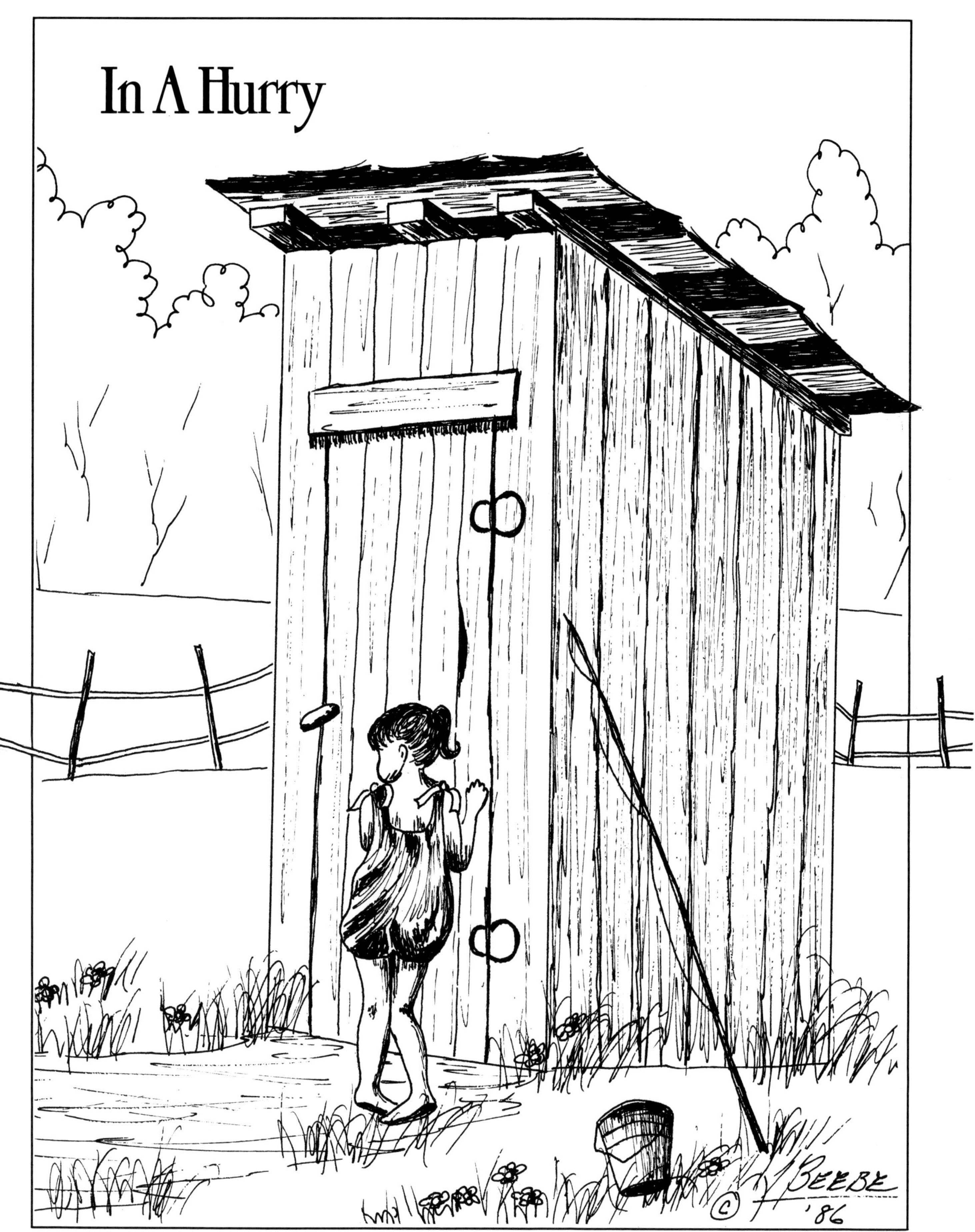

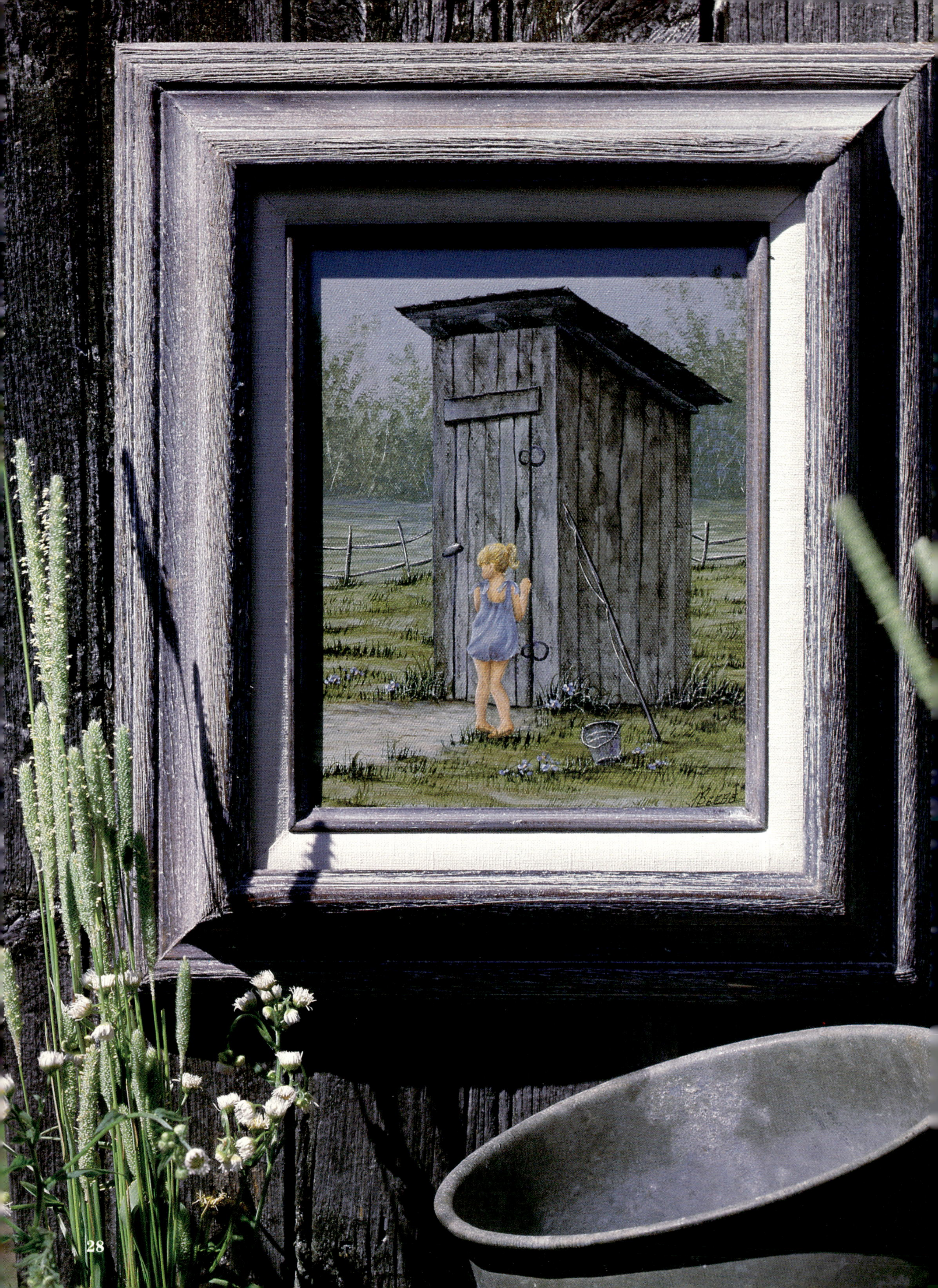

# In A Hurry

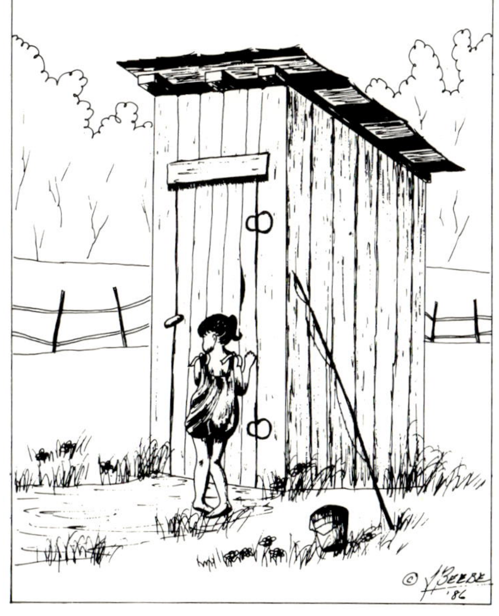

**CANVAS:** 8″ x 10″ stretched portrait smooth canvas.

**PALETTE:** **Permalba Tube Acrylics;** Cobalt Blue, Mars Black, Burnt Umber, Burnt Sienna, Olive Green, Yellow Ochre. Liquitex Gesso. **Folk Art Acrylics;** Skintone, Primrose, Barnwood.

## PAINTING INSTRUCTIONS

### A. SKY:
1. Apply a coat of Medium Mix to the sky area using a 1″ brush.
2. Brush in a Mix I WASH.

### B. BACKGROUND FIELD AND FOLIAGE:
1. Dab in foliage in CREAMY CONSISTENCY Mix II. Dab it out with a DAMP brush.
2. Intensify with an Olive Green WASH.
3. Dampen and scratch out a suggestion of tree branches.
4. Paint the field in a Mix II WASH streaked horizontally.
5. Highlight with a Mix I GLAZE.

### C. OUTHOUSE:
1. Establish the outhouse in a RUNNING WASH of Mix III.
2. Add line work of INK CONSISTENCY Mix III.
3. Shadow with a Mix III GLAZE.
4. Accent with a Mix I GLAZE.
5. Highlight with a Barnwood WASH.

### D. PATH:
1. Establish the path in a Skintone WASH.
2. Shade with a Burnt Umber GLAZE.

### E. GROUND:
1. Establish the ground in an Olive Green WASH streaked horizontally.
2. Wisp up grass of INK CONSISTENCY Olive Green using the fan brush.
3. Add INK CONSISTENCY Olive Green liner grass.
4. Dampen and scratch out highlight grass.

### F. LITTLE GIRL:
1. Basecoat the flesh areas with Skintone.
2. Shade with a Mix IV WASH, corner loaded.
3. Accent with a Primrose GLAZE.
4. Highlight with a Gesso WASH, corner loaded.
5. Basecoat the hair with Yellow Ochre.
6. Shade with a Burnt Umber WASH, corner loaded.
7. Highlight with Yellow Ochre + Gesso (1:2) (light yellow).

### G. CLOTHING AND FLOWERS:
1. Basecoat the sunsuit with Mix I.
2. Paint the flowers in Mix I using the tip of a liner brush.
3. Shade with a Mix III WASH, corner loaded.
4. Highlight with a Gesso WASH.
5. Accent with a Cobalt Blue GLAZE.

### H. FENCE, PAIL AND FISHPOLE:
1. Basecoat with Barnwood.
2. Shade with Mix III, corner loaded.
3. Dampen and scratch out highlights.
4. Accent the pail with a Cobalt Blue GLAZE.

# Teddy's Hour

**CANVAS:** 12″ x 16″ stretched portrait smooth canvas.

**PALETTE:** **Permalba Tube Acrylics;** Yellow Ochre, Burnt Umber, Mars Black, Alizarin Crimson. **Folk Art Acrylics;** Slate Blue, Skintone.

## BACKGROUND:

**1.** Select a piece of fabric with a small foral and stripe design in colors that you prefer. The fabric should be a fine, smooth weave.
**2.** Cut the fabric about an inch larger than the canvas.
**3.** Sand the canvas with a piece of fine sandpaper.
**4.** With a 1″ inch sponge brush, apply a coat of acrylic Matte Medium. Position the fabric, smooth it down and immediately apply a coat of acrylic Matte Medium over it.
**5.** Allow to dry and sand lightly. Mark off the border and trace the outline of the design.
**6.** Undercoat the entire bear, lamb and jacks in Gesso. Allow to dry and retransfer the design lines.
**7.** Paint the border in an acrylic color to match the background of the fabric using a 1″ sponge brush (Skintone).
**8.** Stripe the border with Mix I and Mix II which will be mixes made to match the two main colors of your fabric choice.

## PAINTING INSTRUCTIONS

### A. BEAR:

**1.** Basecoat with Yellow Ochre.
**2.** Shade with a Burnt Umber WASH.
**3.** Intensify with a Mix III GLAZE.
**4.** Highlight with Skintone.
**5.** Paint the eyes, nose and mouth with Mars Black.
**6.** Highlight the eyes with Gesso.

### B. LAMB:

**1.** Basecoat the face, ear and legs with Mars Black.
**2.** Highlight with a Gesso WASH.
**3.** Basecoat the lamb with Gesso.
**4.** Shade with a Slate Blue WASH, corner loaded.
**5.** Paint heart with Mix II.
**6.** Shade heart and paint ribbon with the dark color from Mix II (Alizarin Crimson + Burnt Umber).
**7.** Paint cast shadows with a Mix III GLAZE.

### C. RIBBON, BASE OF LAMB AND JACKS:

**1.** Basecoat in Mix I.
**2.** Shade with a Mix III WASH, corner loaded.
**3.** Highlight with Gesso.

### D. DETAILS:

**1.** Basecoat the flower in Mix II.
**2.** Shade with the dark color from Mix II ( Alizarin Crimson + Burnt Umber).
**3.** Shadow three corners of the background with a Mix III GLAZE.
**4.** Cast shadows from the jacks onto the surface and from the bear and lamb onto the background using a Mix III GLAZE.

**Note:** Amy's Hour is featured in *The Joy of Canvas Painting* by Joyce Beebe.

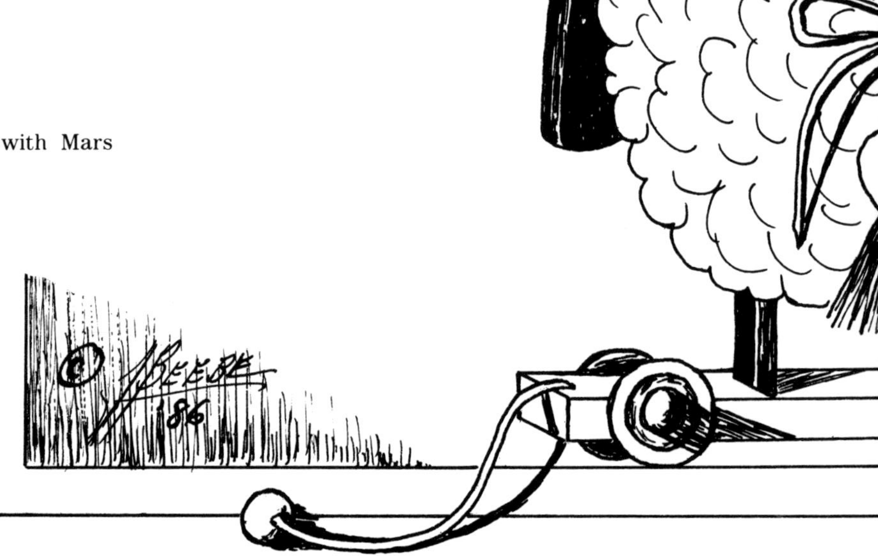

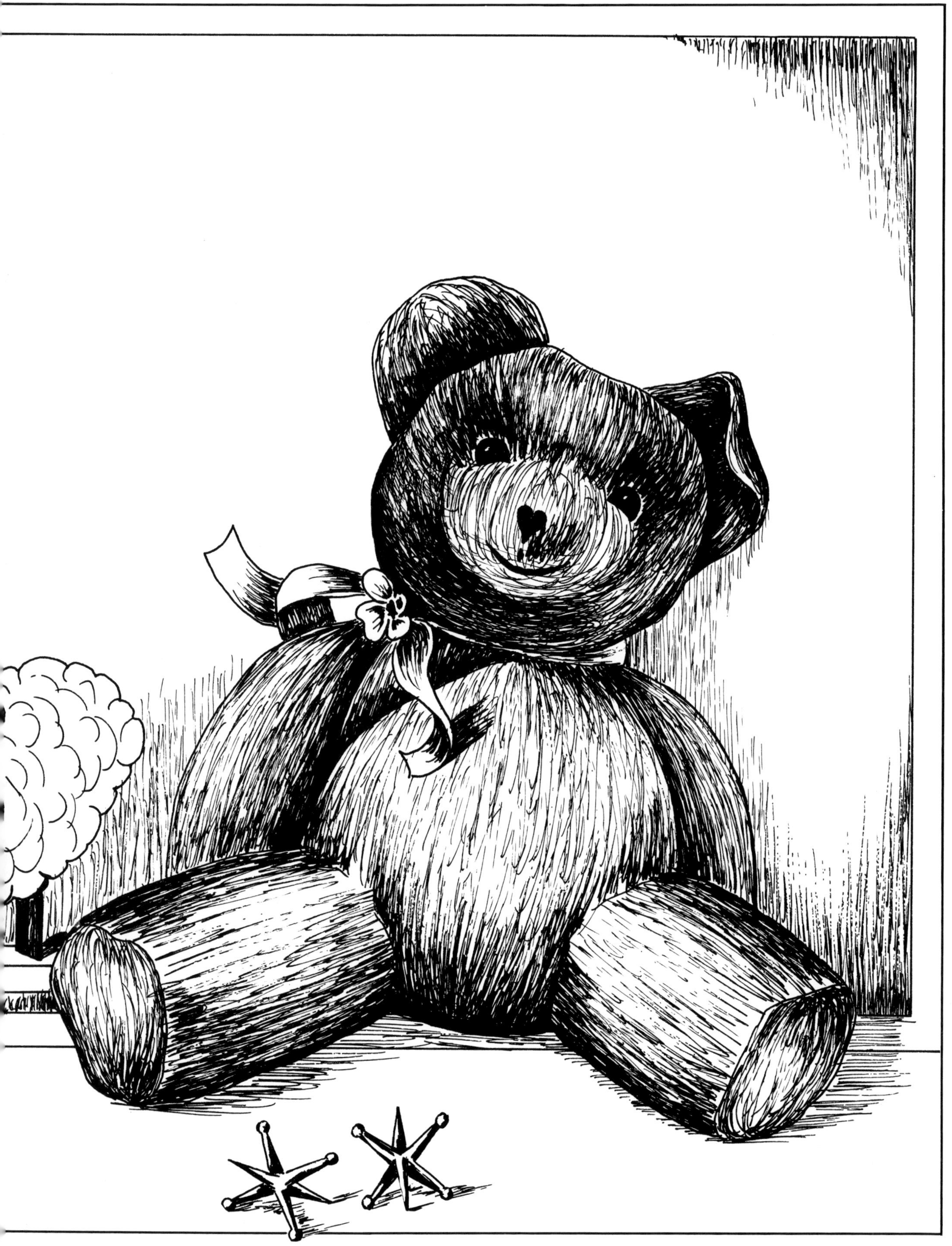

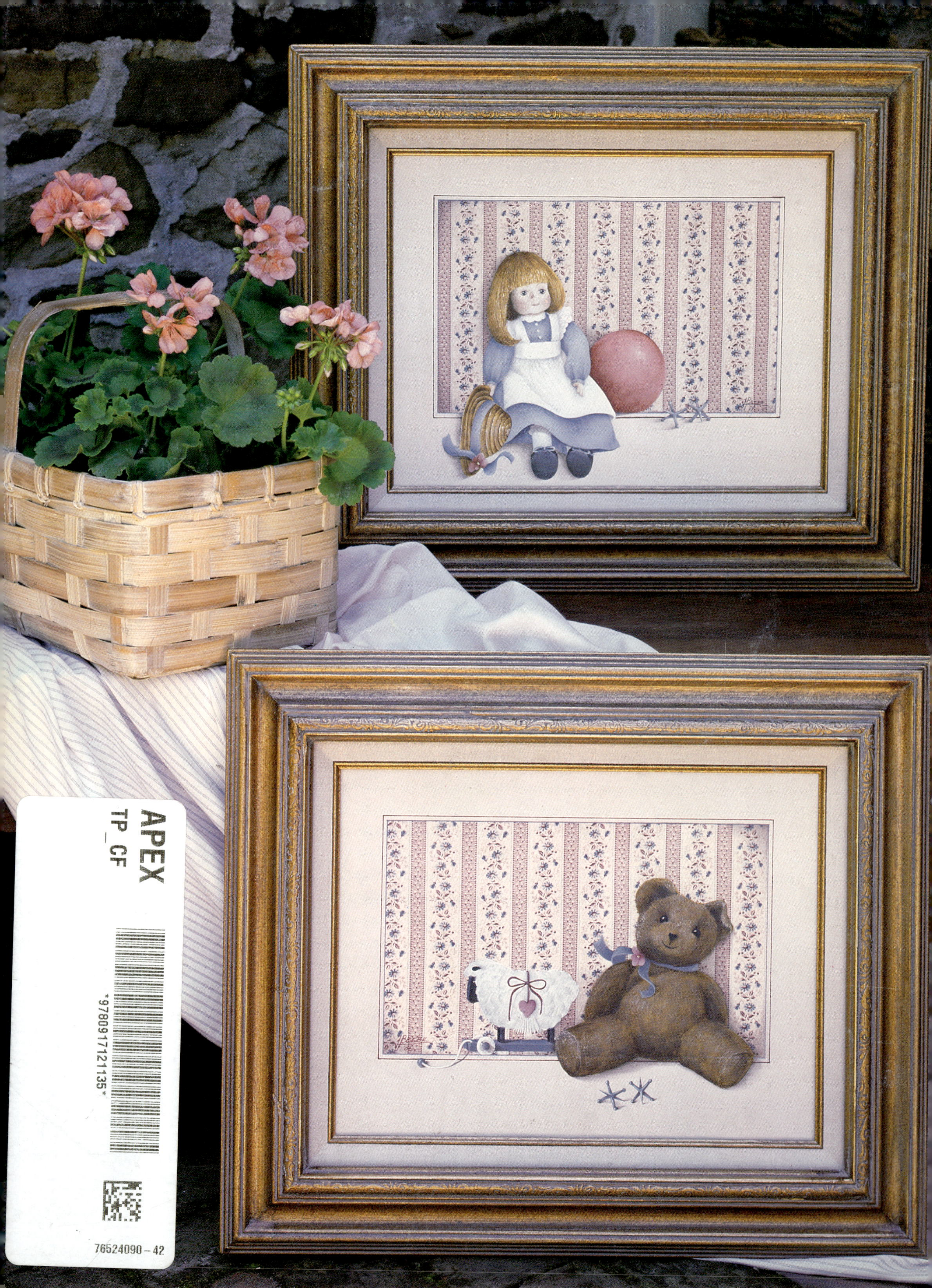
APEX
TP_CF
9780917121135
76524090 - 42